BOOK #1
9 781971 801001
AF225881
DVI
Imfamou$
Tea
U HAVE BEEN
T-BAGGED
IMFAMOUS

# THE HOLE SCHOOL OF ART

IN THE BELLY OF OLD WEST HALL AT D.V.I., THERE'S A PLACE WHERE THE AIR IS THIN AND THE SILENCE IS HEAVY. THEY CALL IT THE HOLE. MOST MEN GO THERE TO BREAK. I WENT THERE BECAUSE HAD NO OTHER CHOICE, BUT I DIDN'T GO ALONE.

RICH "IMFAMOUS" COMPTON STEPPED INTO THAT DARKNESS WITH ME.

HE DIDN'T HAVE TO BE THERE, BUT HE REFUSED TO LET A 19-YEAR-OLD KID FACE THE "BATTLE" ALONE. WHILE THE WORLD OUTSIDE FORGOT WE EXISTED, HE PUT A PENCIL IN MY HAND. HE TAUGHT ME THAT YOUR MIND DOESN'T HAVE A CAGE UNLESS YOU BUILD ONE. HE TAUGHT ME TO DRAW, TO THINK, AND TO STAY SOLID WHEN THE WALLS CLOSE IN. THIS ISN'T JUST A BOOK OF DRAWINGS. IT'S THE CURRICULUM OF A MAN WHO TURNED THE HOLE INTO AN ART STUDIO.

~CODY

# Official Copyright Notice



**Expanded Intellectual Property Statement "Reservation of Rights"**

*Notice of Intellectual Property Rights*:

The title "U have Been T-BAGGED," all associated logos, original illustrations, character designs, and the IMFAMOUS brand identity are the exclusive property of IMFAMOUS LLC. Any unauthorized use of "confusingly similar" names, likenesses, or artistic styles that could cause brand dilution or consumer confusion is strictly prohibited. We reserve the right to take legal action against any party that infringes upon these creative assets or attempts to pass off derivative works as official IMFAMOUS products.

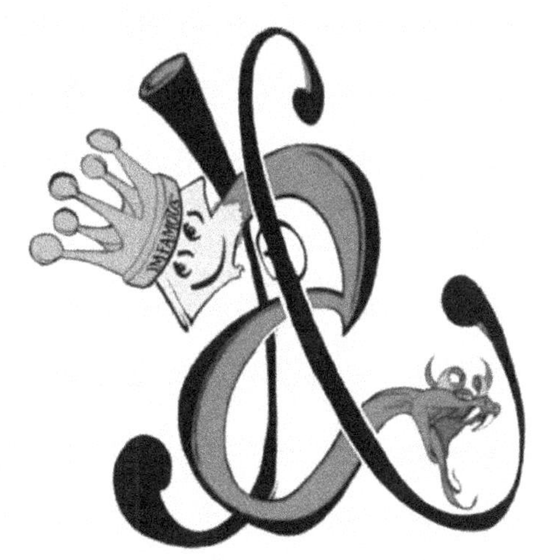

# IF YOU DON'T LIKE THIS COLORING BOOK THEN YOU DONT LIKE TO COLOR

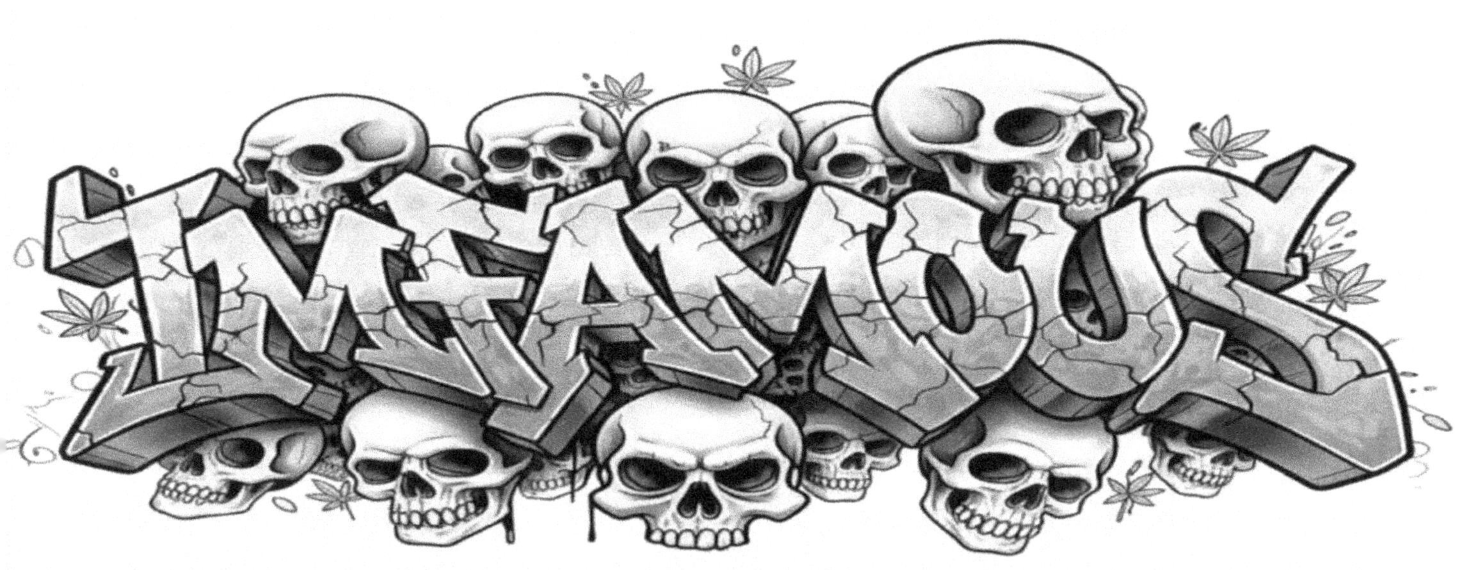

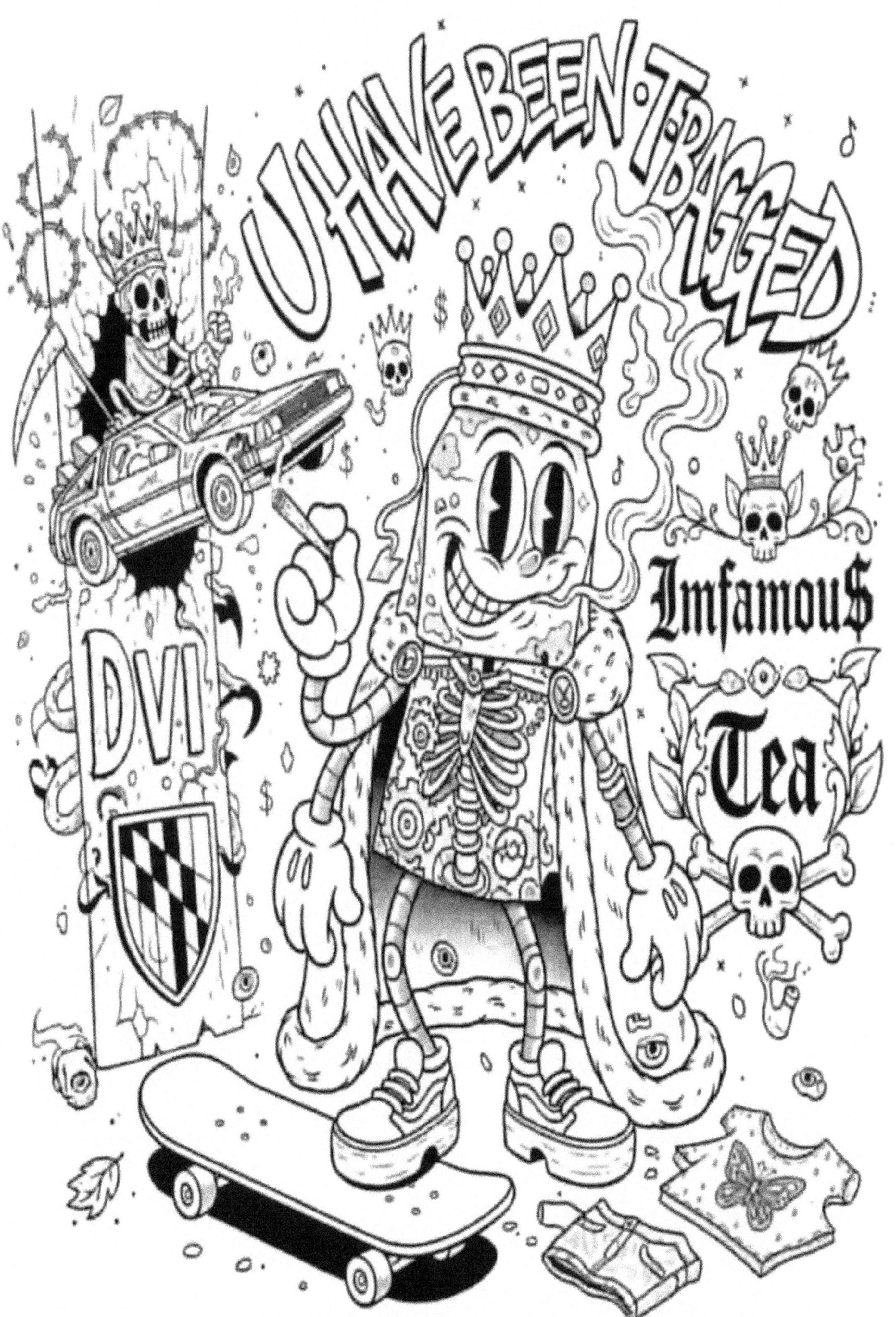
U HAVE BEEN T-BAGGED
DVI
Imfamou$
Tea

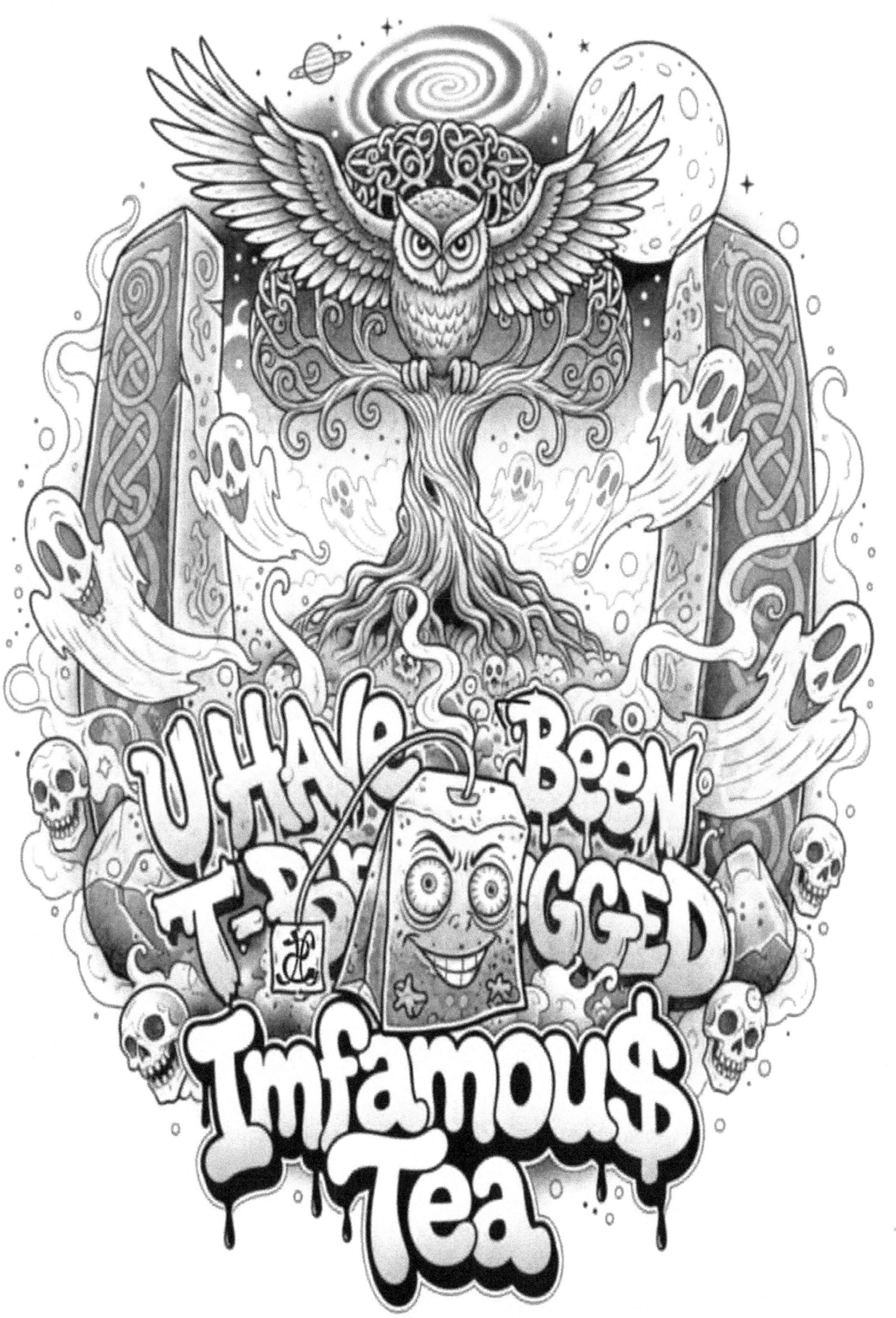
U HAVE BEEN
T-B
GGED
Imfamou$
Tea

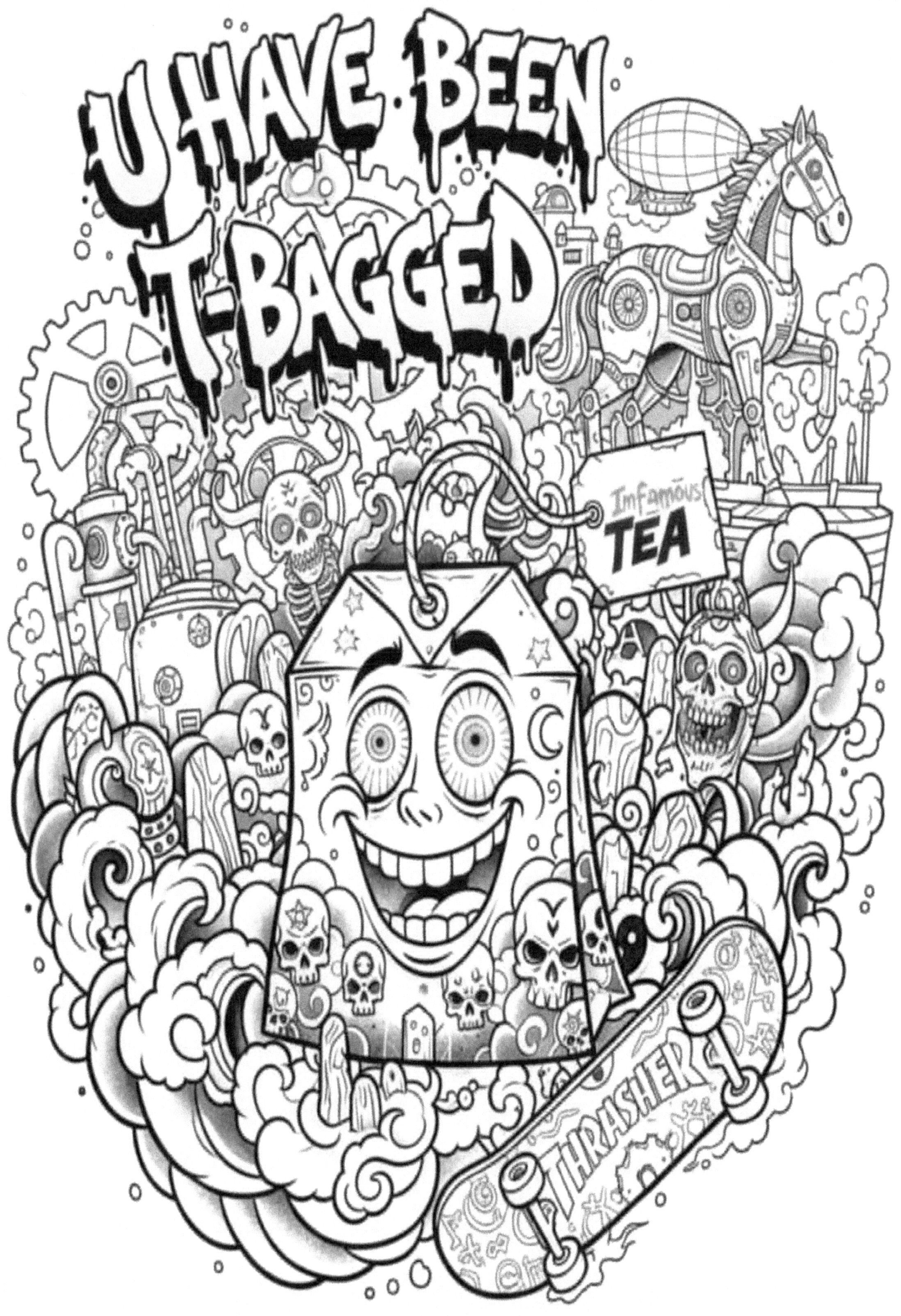
U HAVE BEEN
T-BAGGED
Infamous
TEA
THRASHER

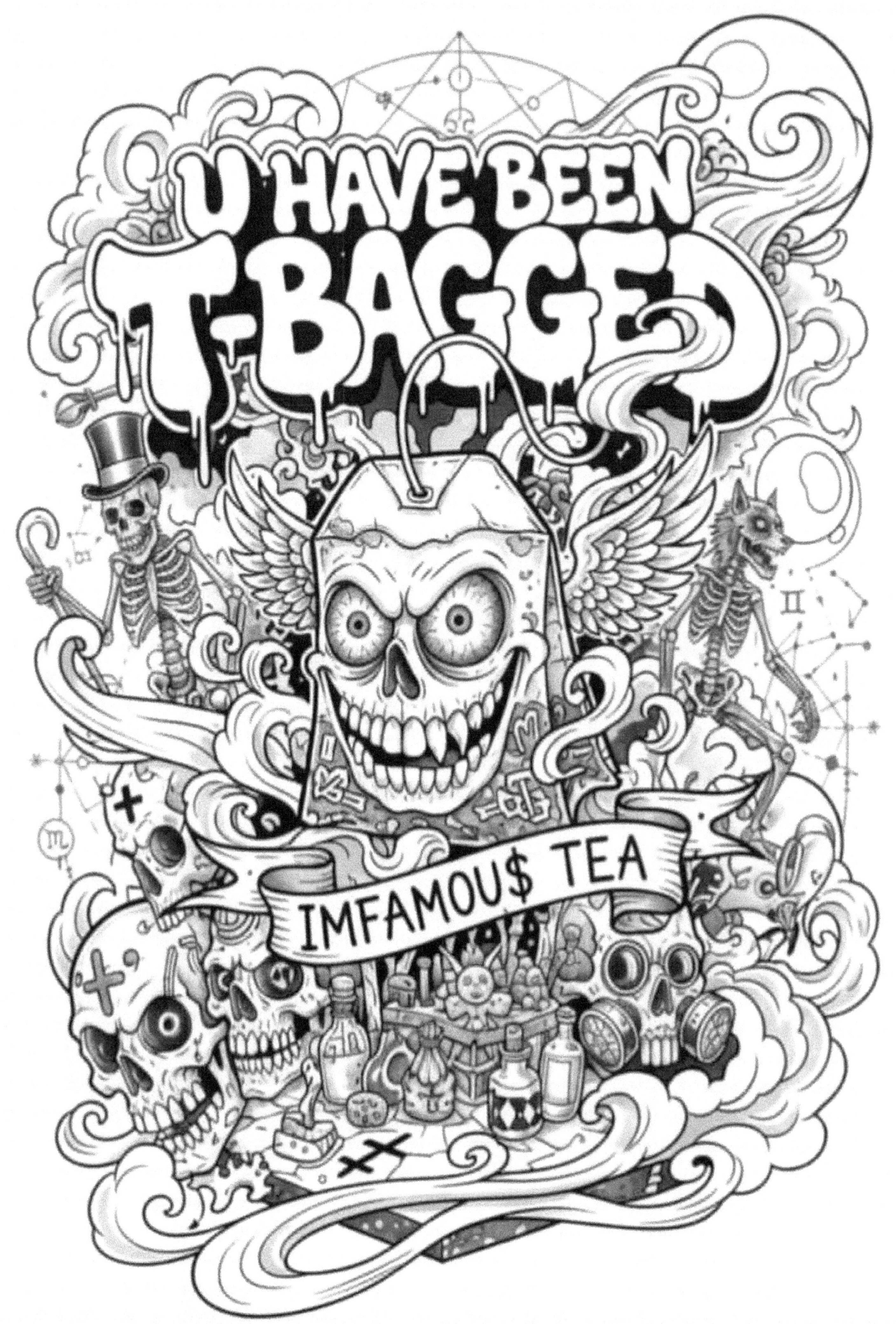
U HAVE BEEN
T-BAGGED
IMFAMOU$ TEA

U HAVE BEEN
T-BAGGED
Imfamous
Tea

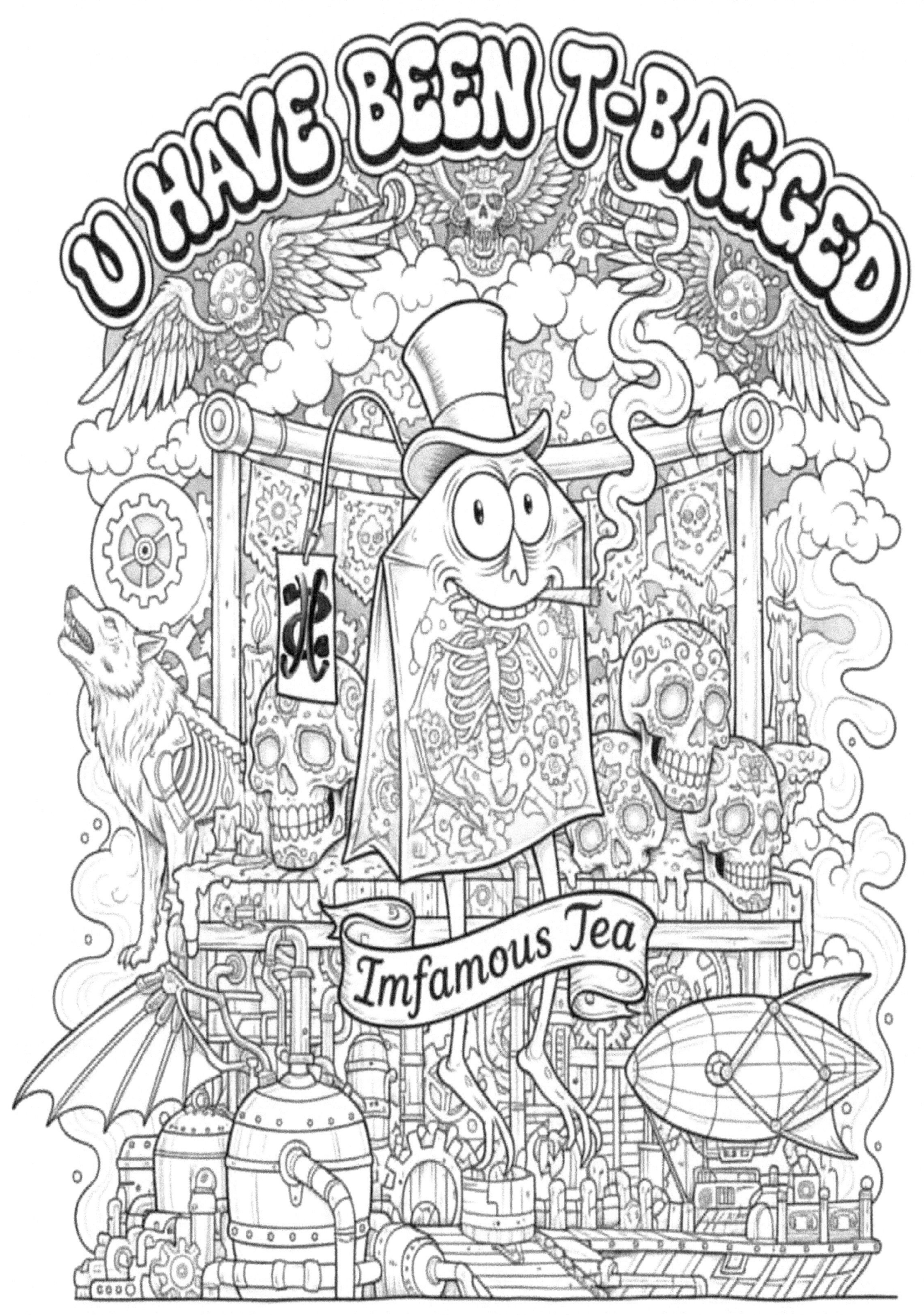
U HAVE BEEN T-BAGGED
Imfamous Tea

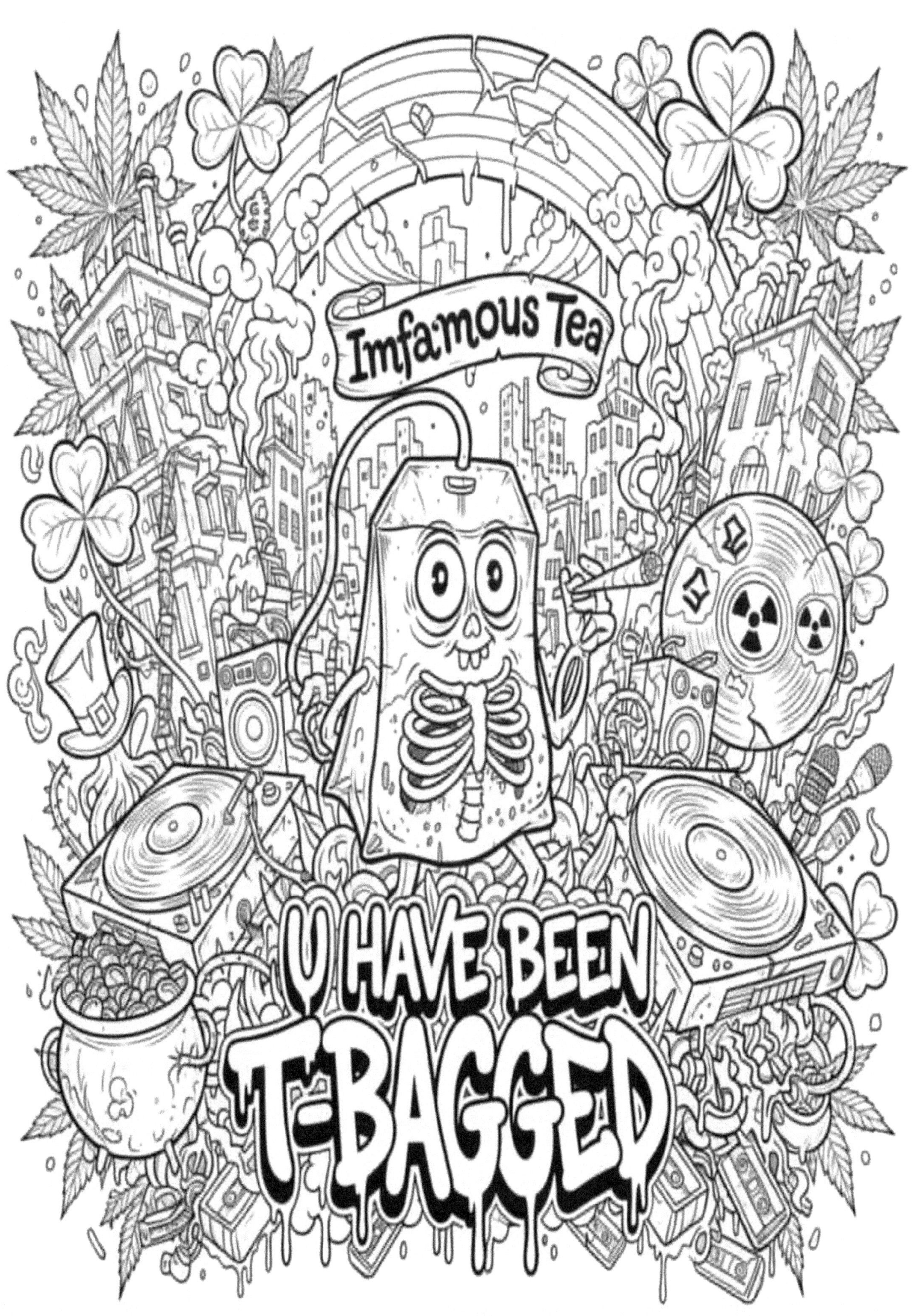
Imfamous Tea
U HAVE BEEN
T-BAGGED

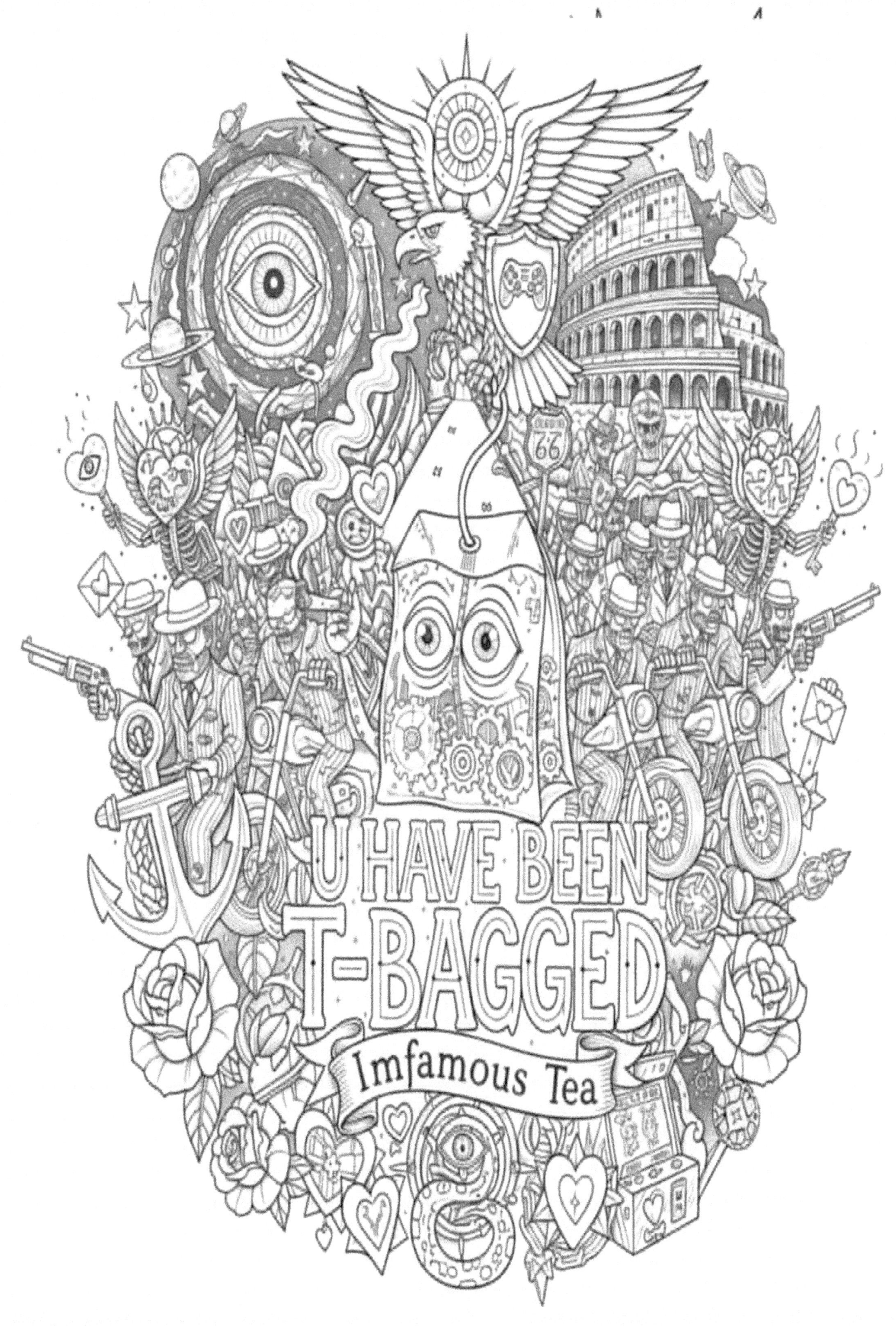

U HAVE BEEN
T-BAGGED
Imfamous Tea
66

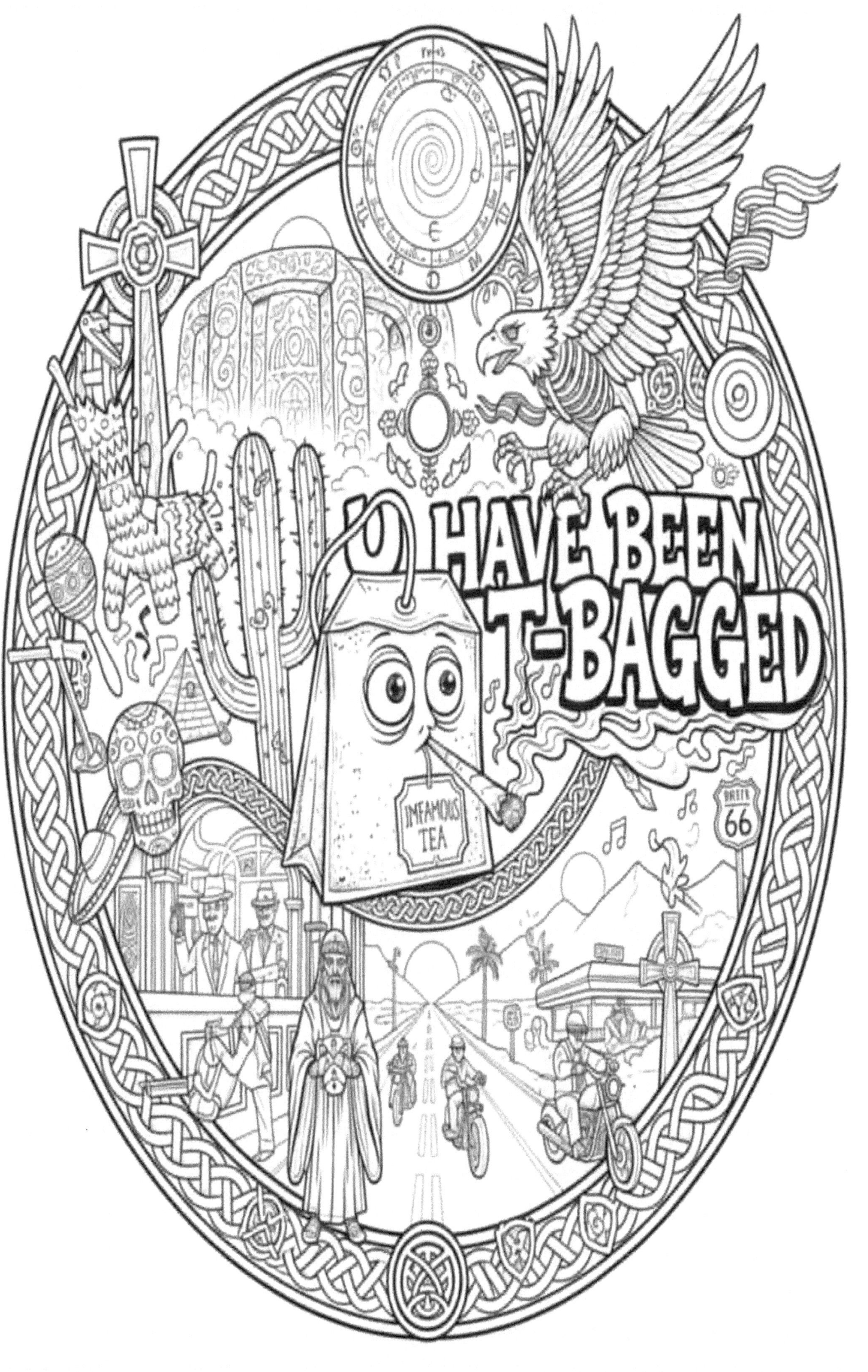
HAVE BEEN
T-BAGGED
INFAMOUS
TEA
66

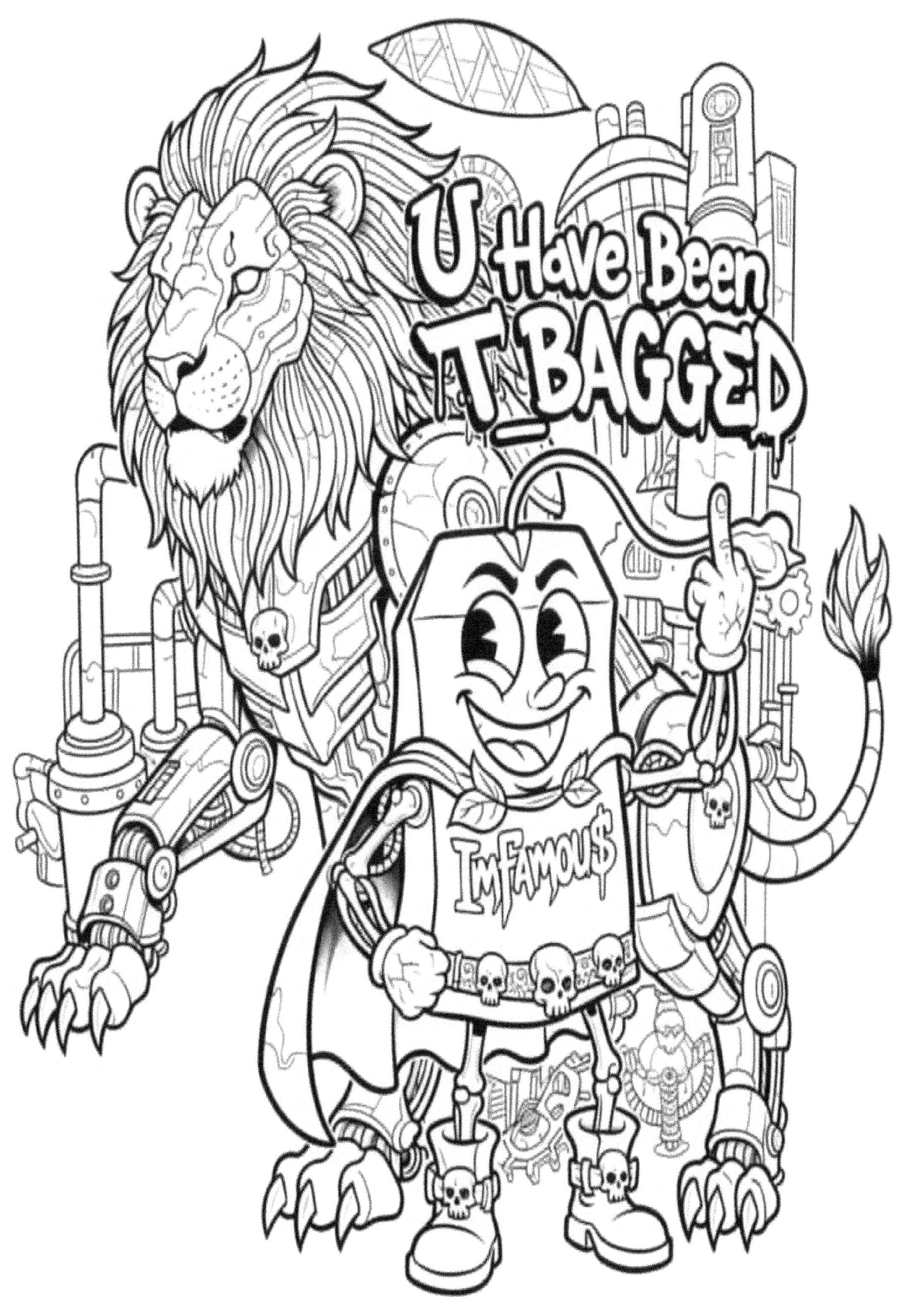
U Have Been
T_BAGGED
I'm FAMOU$

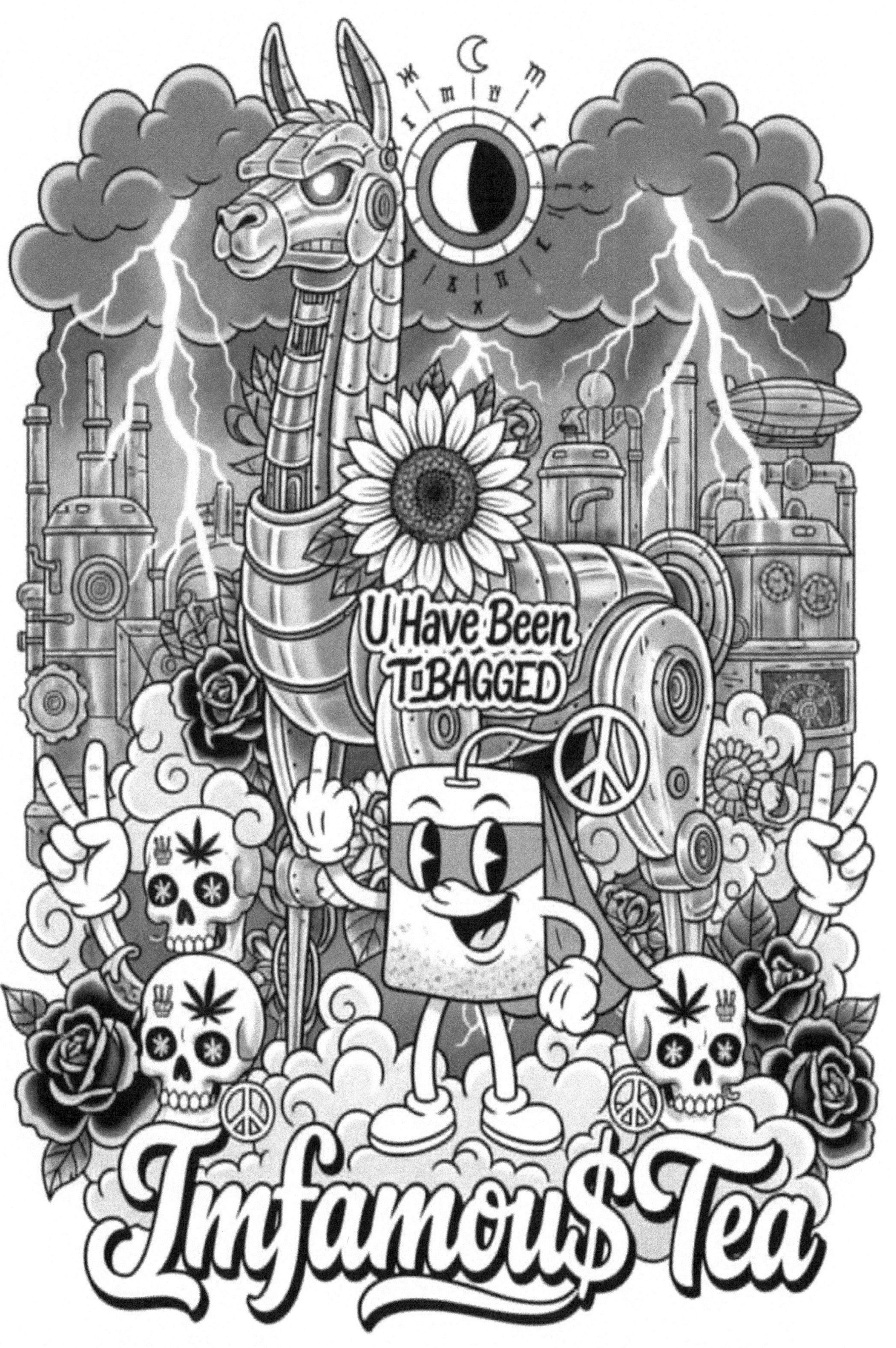

U Have Been
T BAGGED
Imfamou$ Tea

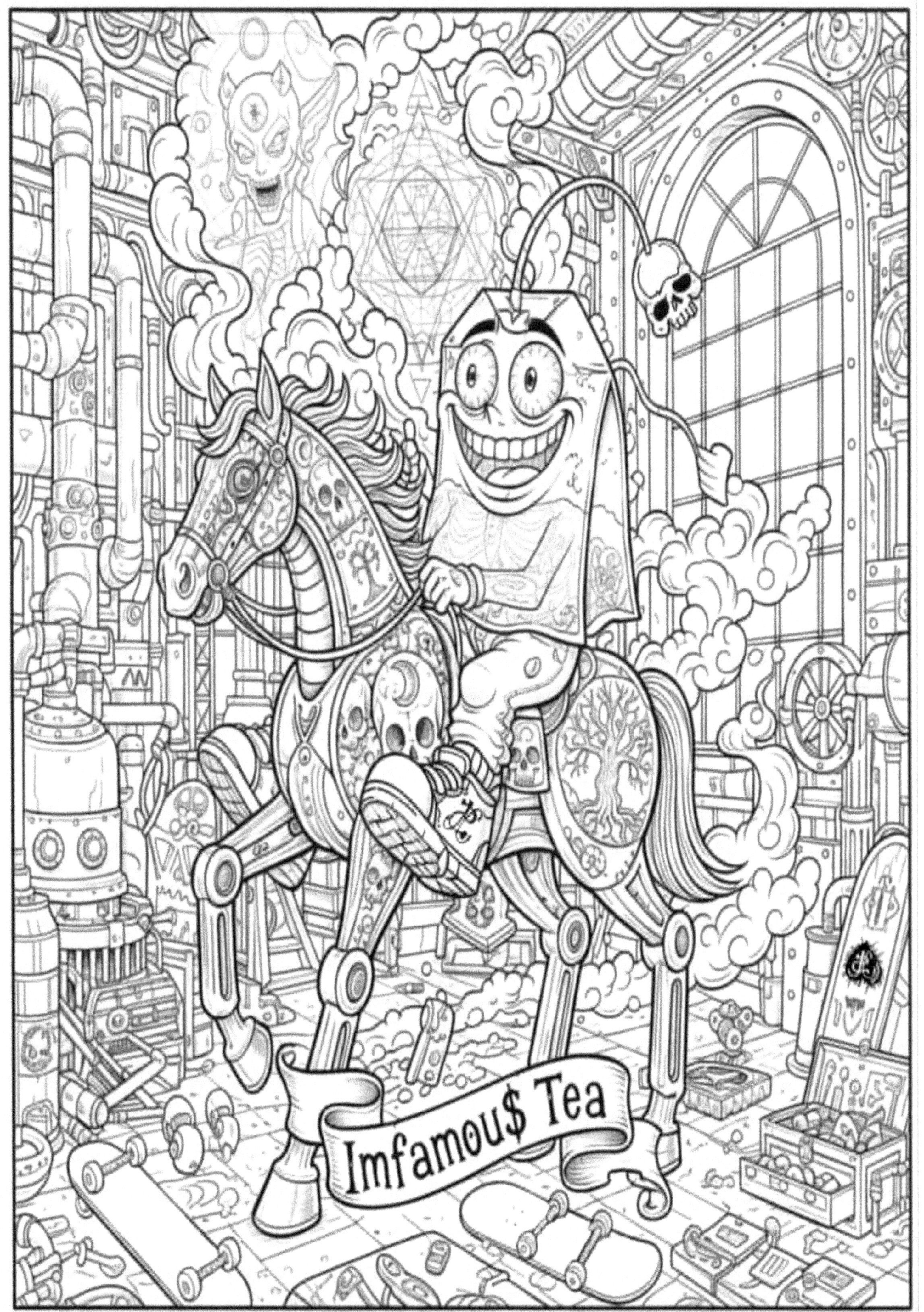
Imfamou$ Tea

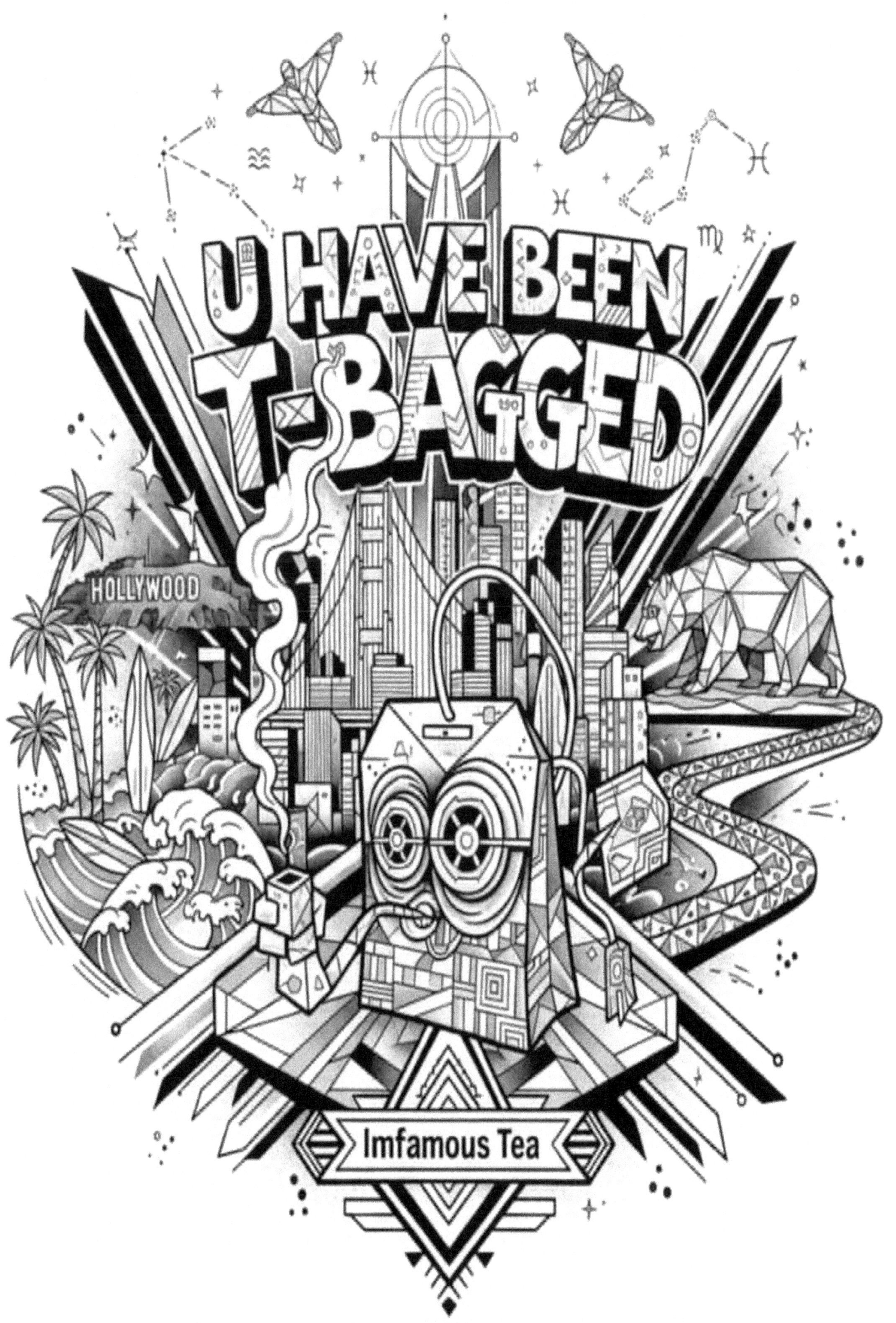
U HAVE BEEN
T-BAGGED
HOLLYWOOD
Imfamous Tea

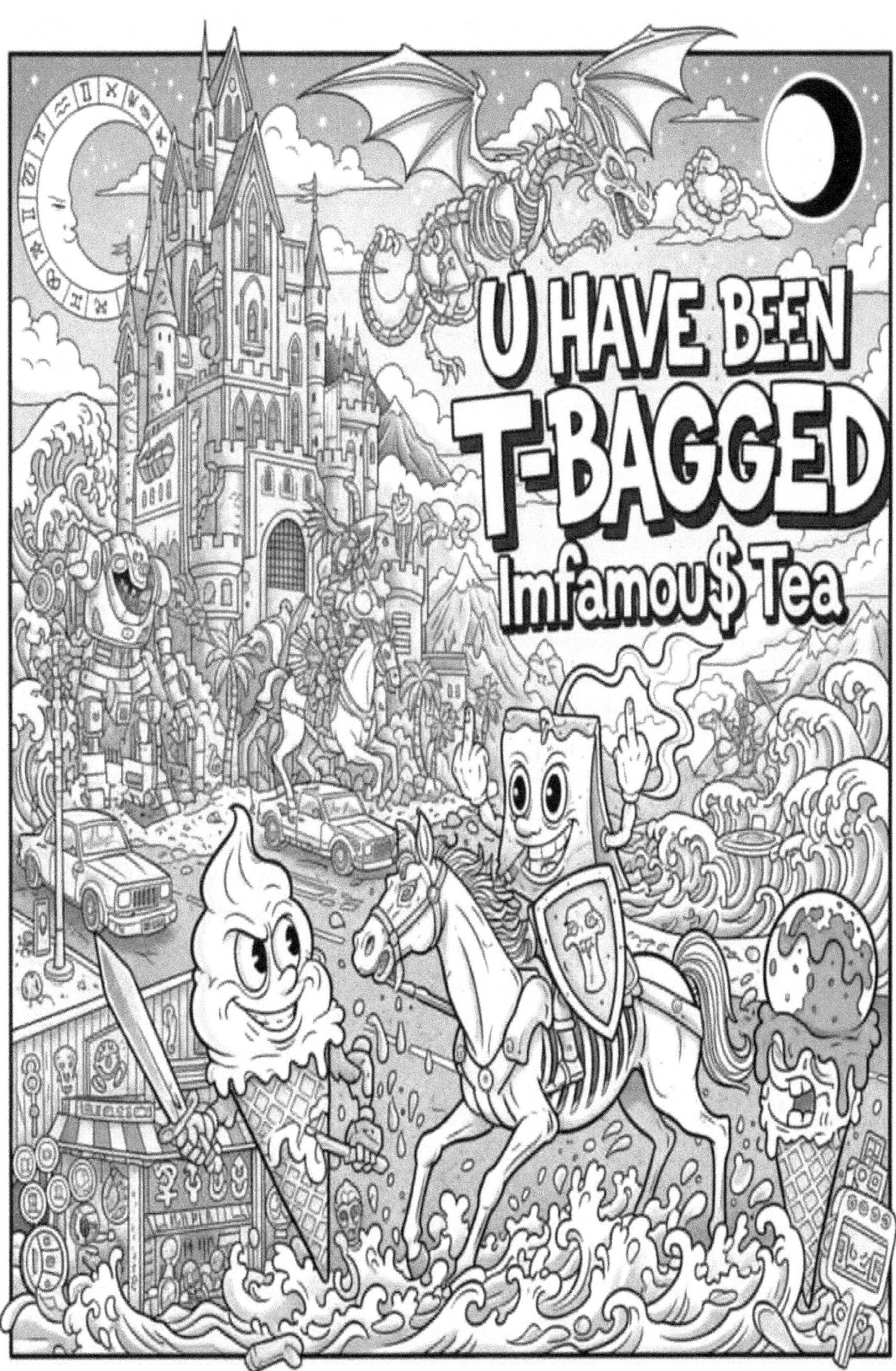
U HAVE BEEN
T-BAGGED
Imfamou$ Tea

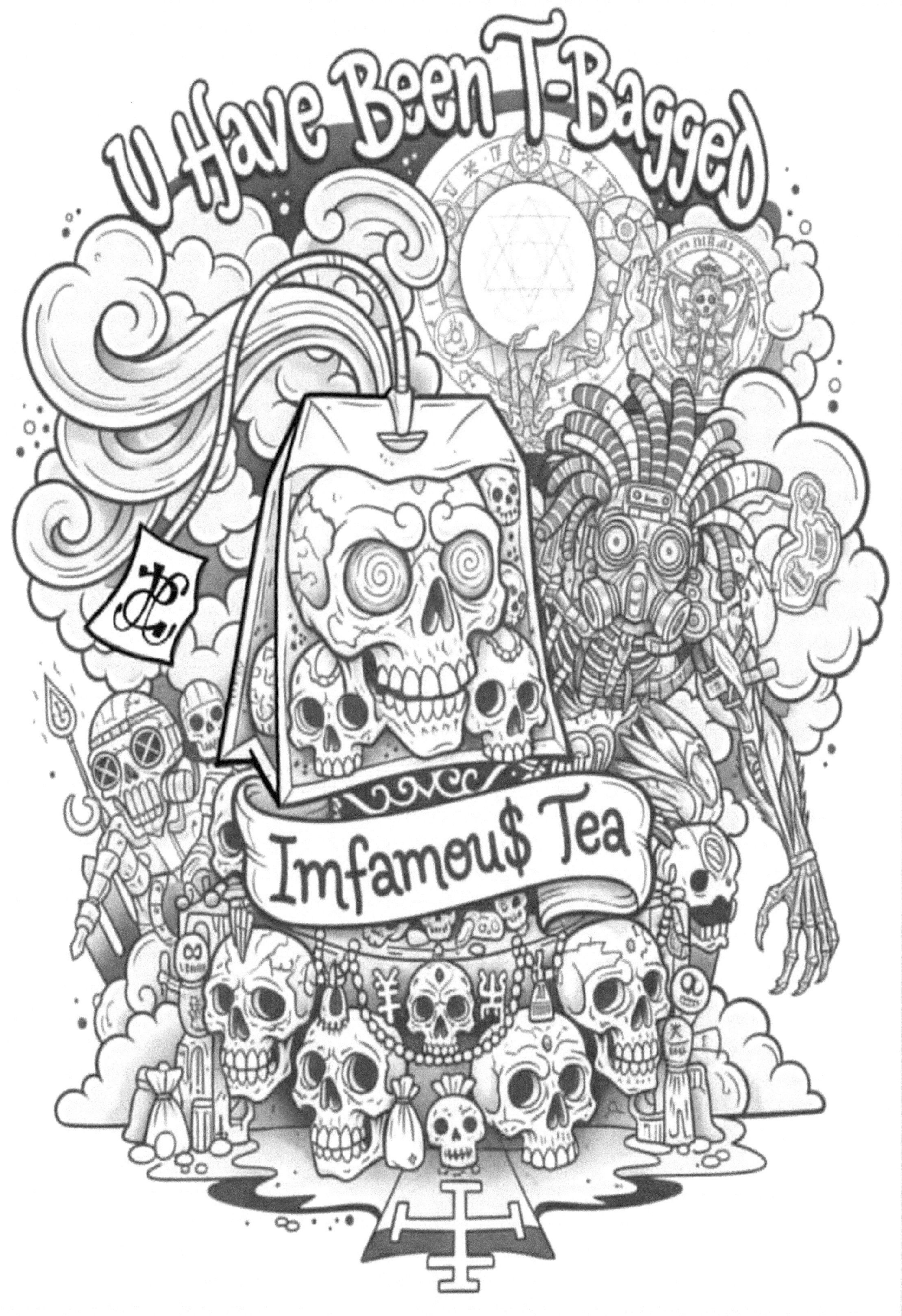
U Have Been T-Bagged
Imfamou$ Tea

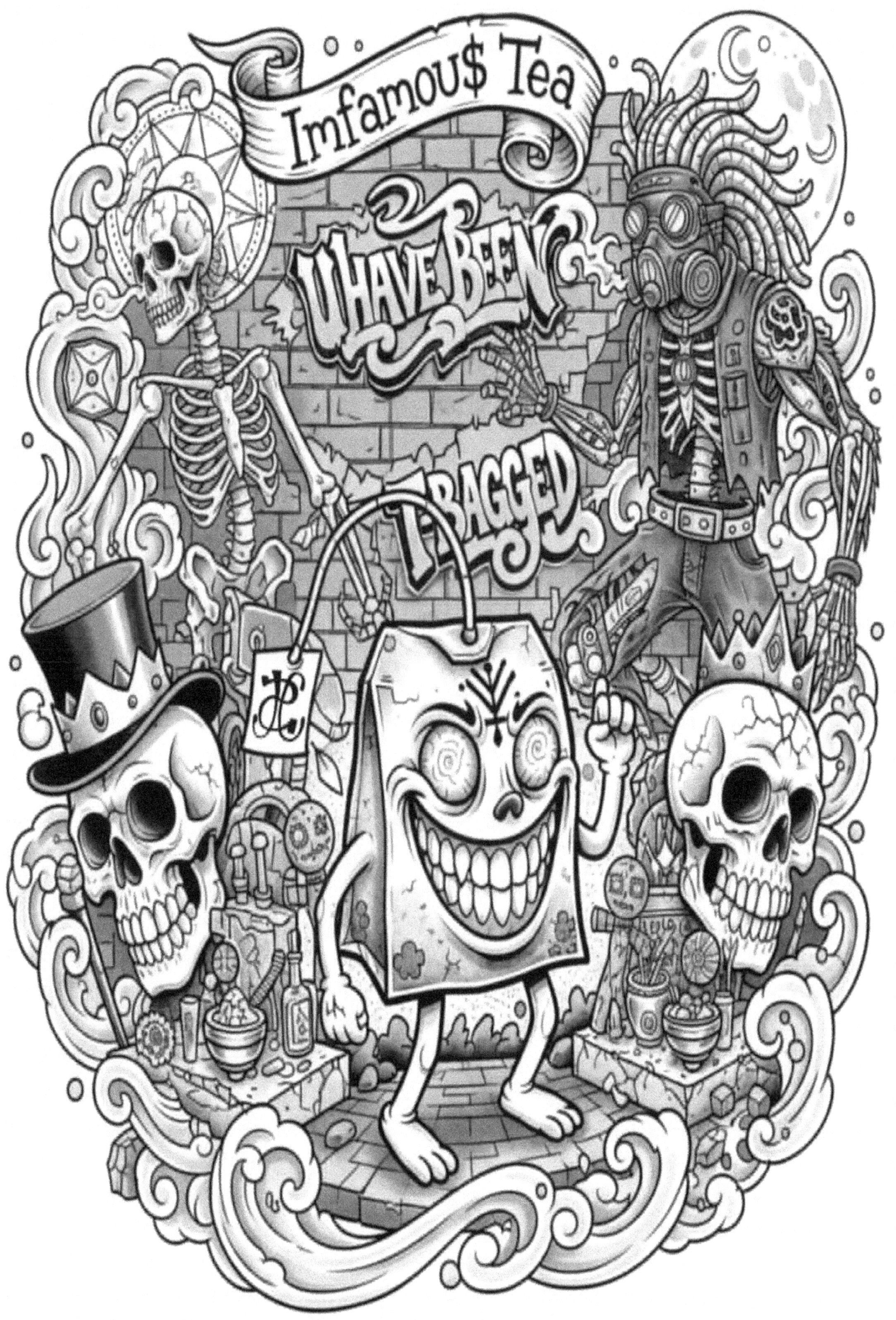
Imfamou$ Tea
U HAVE BEEN
T BAGGED

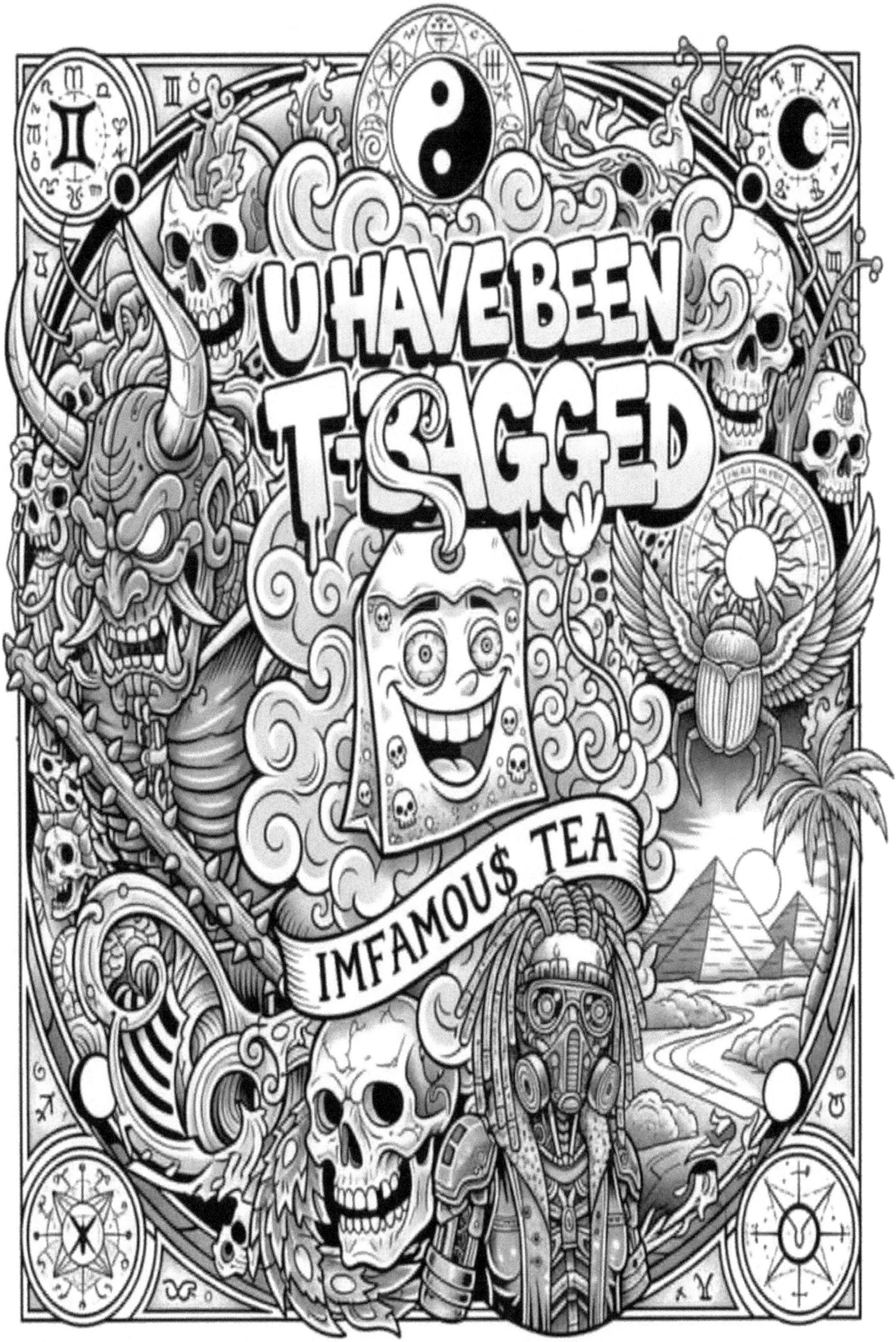
U HAVE BEEN
T-BAGGED
IMFAMOU$ TEA

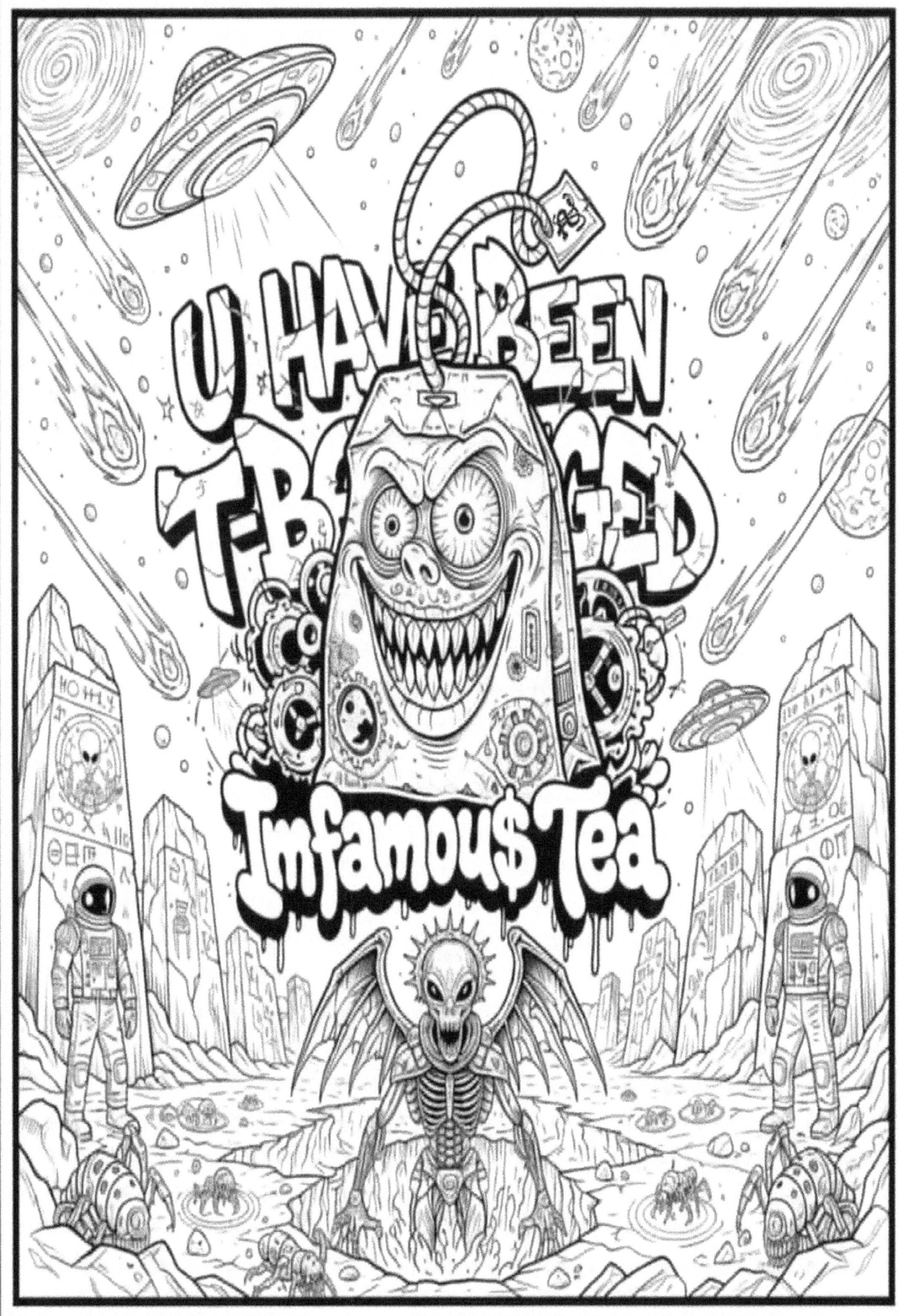
Imfamou$ Tea

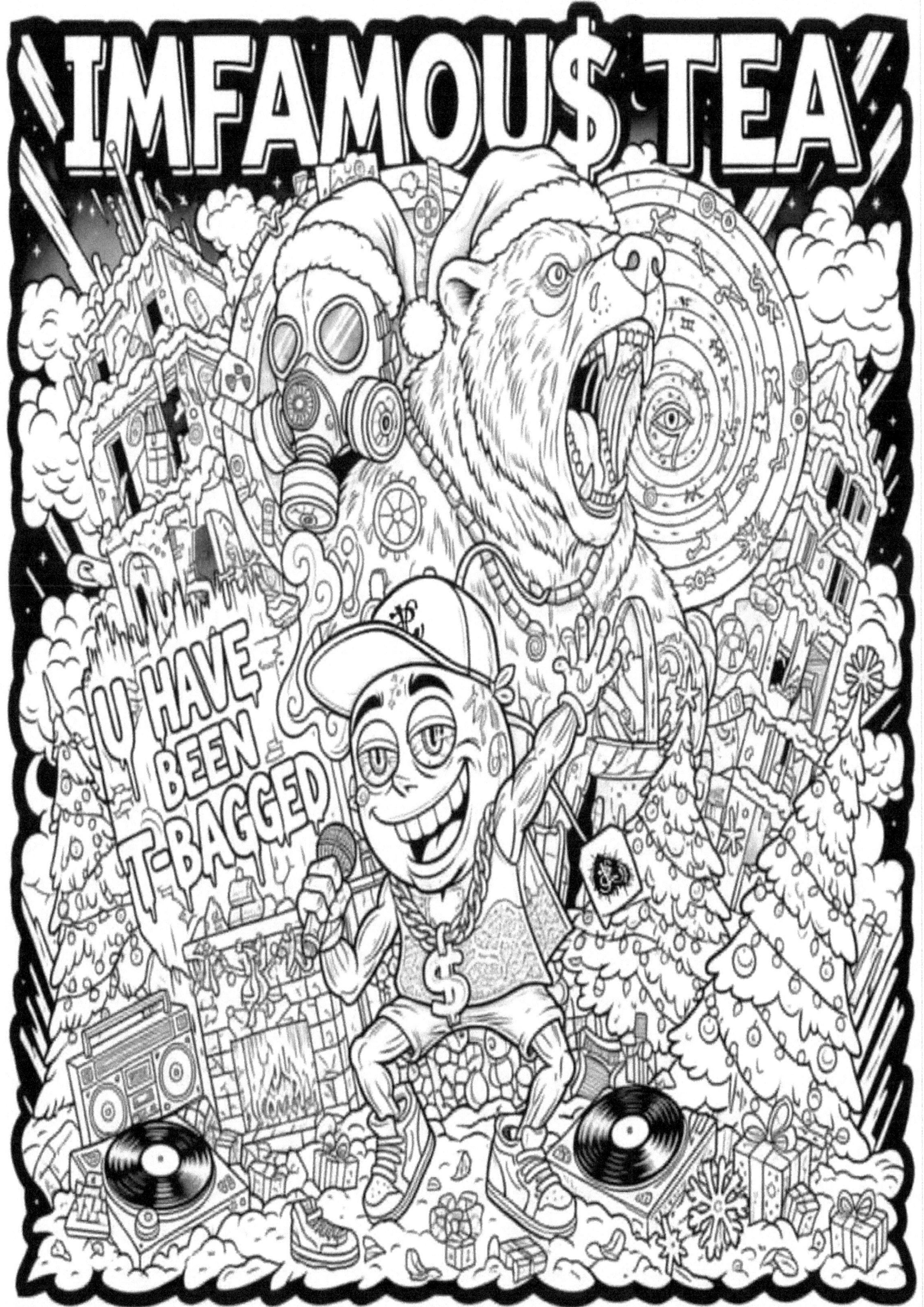

IMFAMOU$ TEA
U HAVE BEEN T-BAGGED

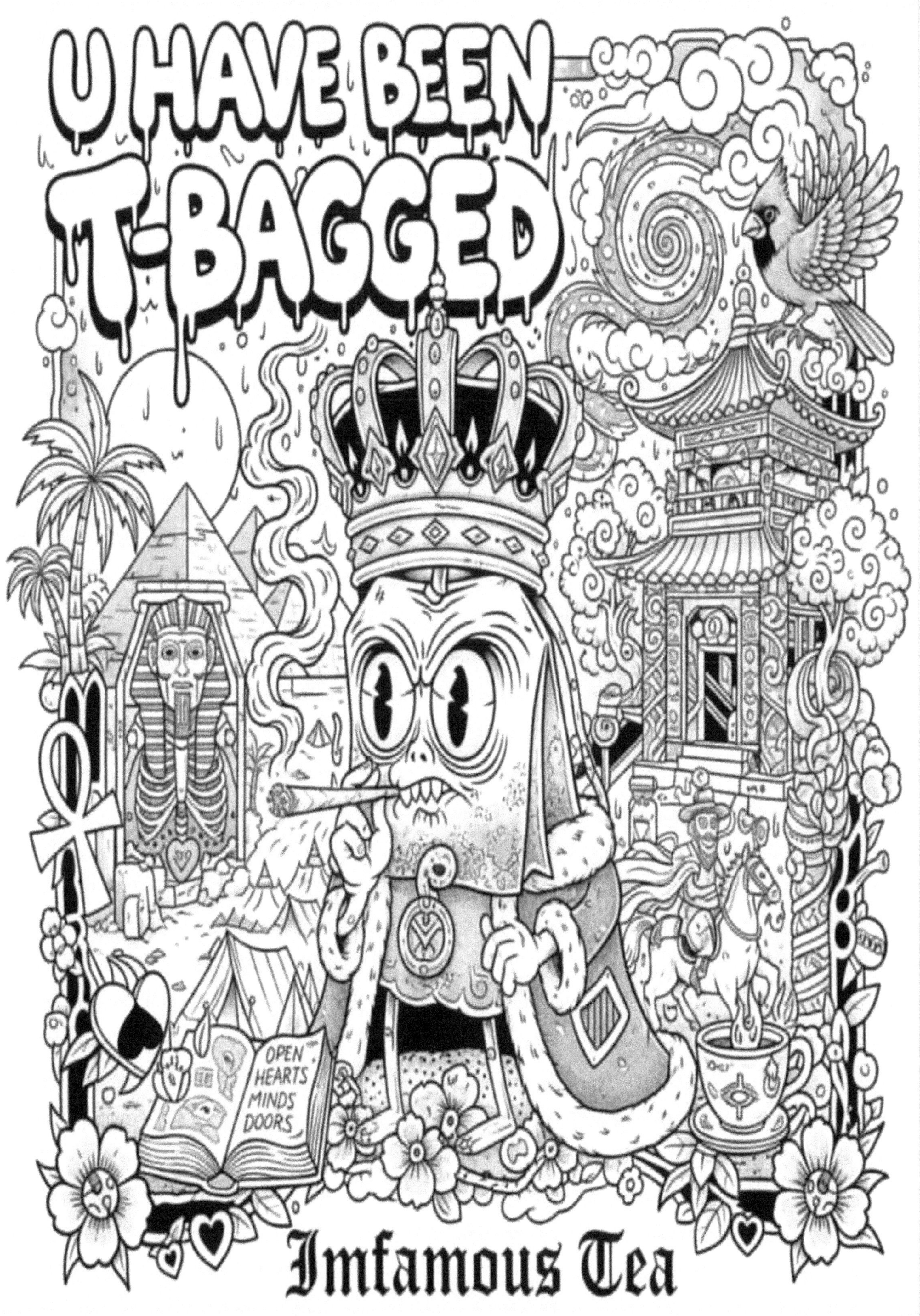
U HAVE BEEN
T-BAGGED
OPEN
HEARTS
MINDS
DOORS
Imfamous Tea

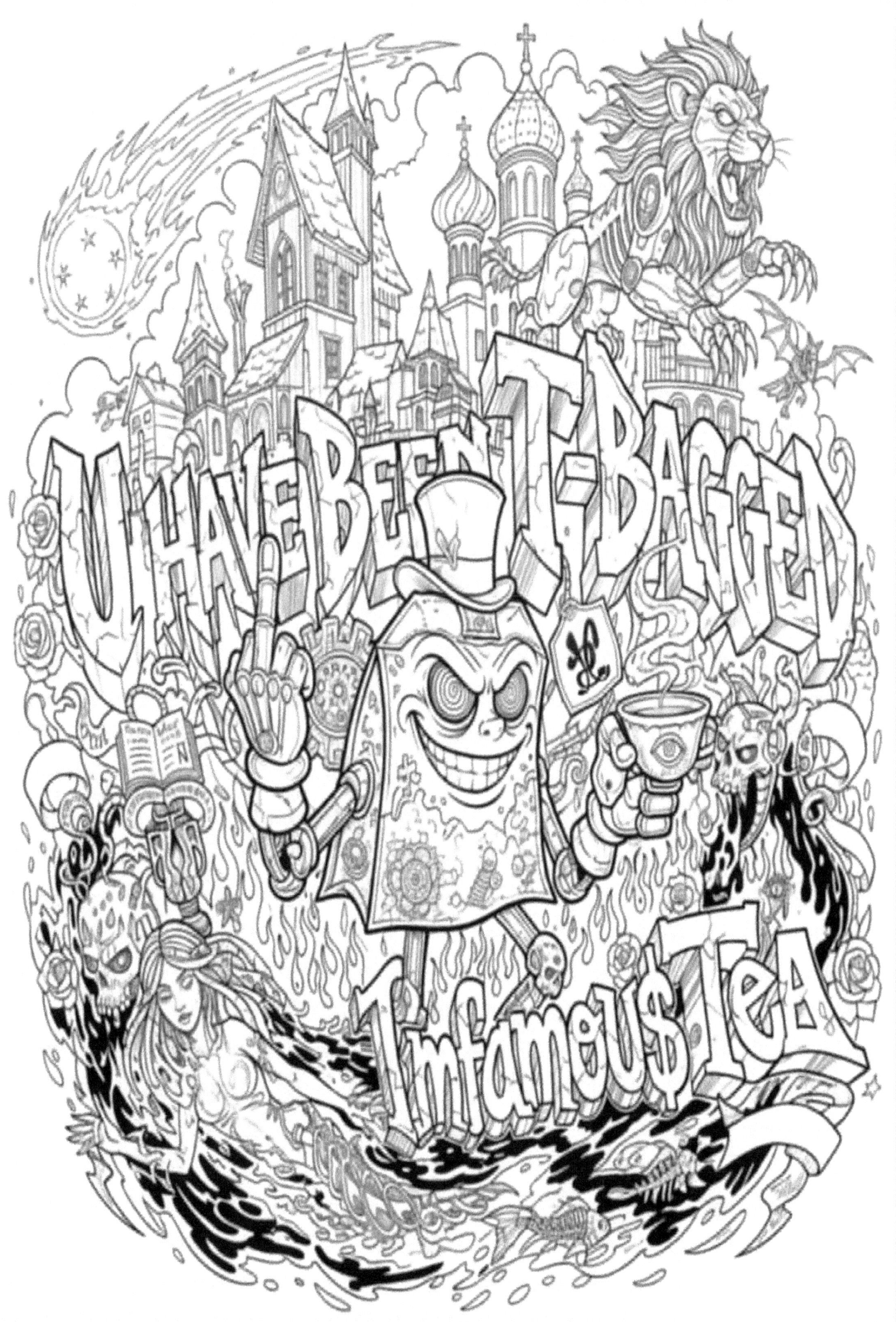
U HAVE BEEN T-BAGGED
Infamou$ Tea

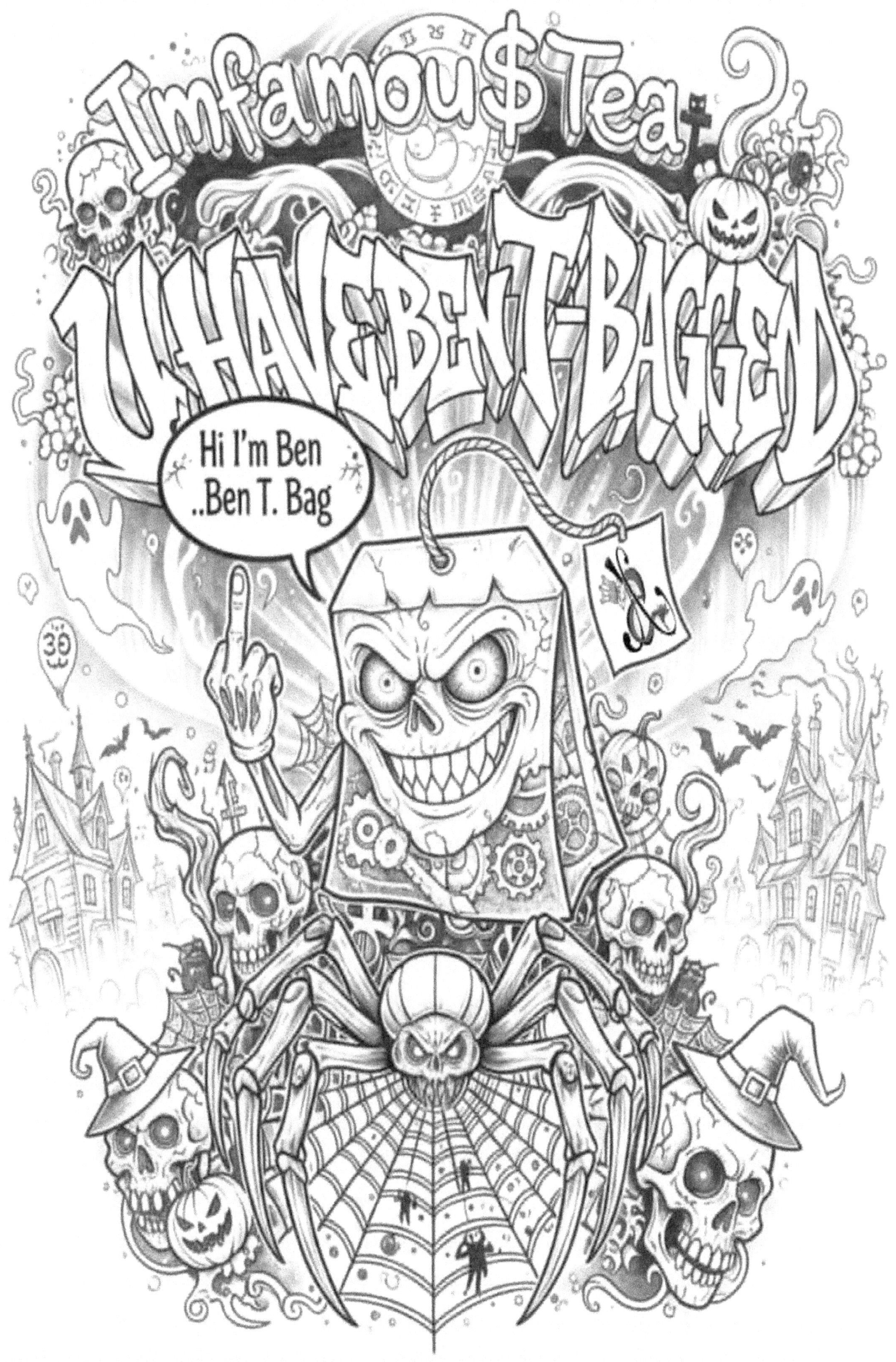
Imfamou$ Tea
UHAVEBENT-BAGGED
Hi I'm Ben
..Ben T. Bag

U Have Ben
T-BaggeD
Imfamou$ Tea

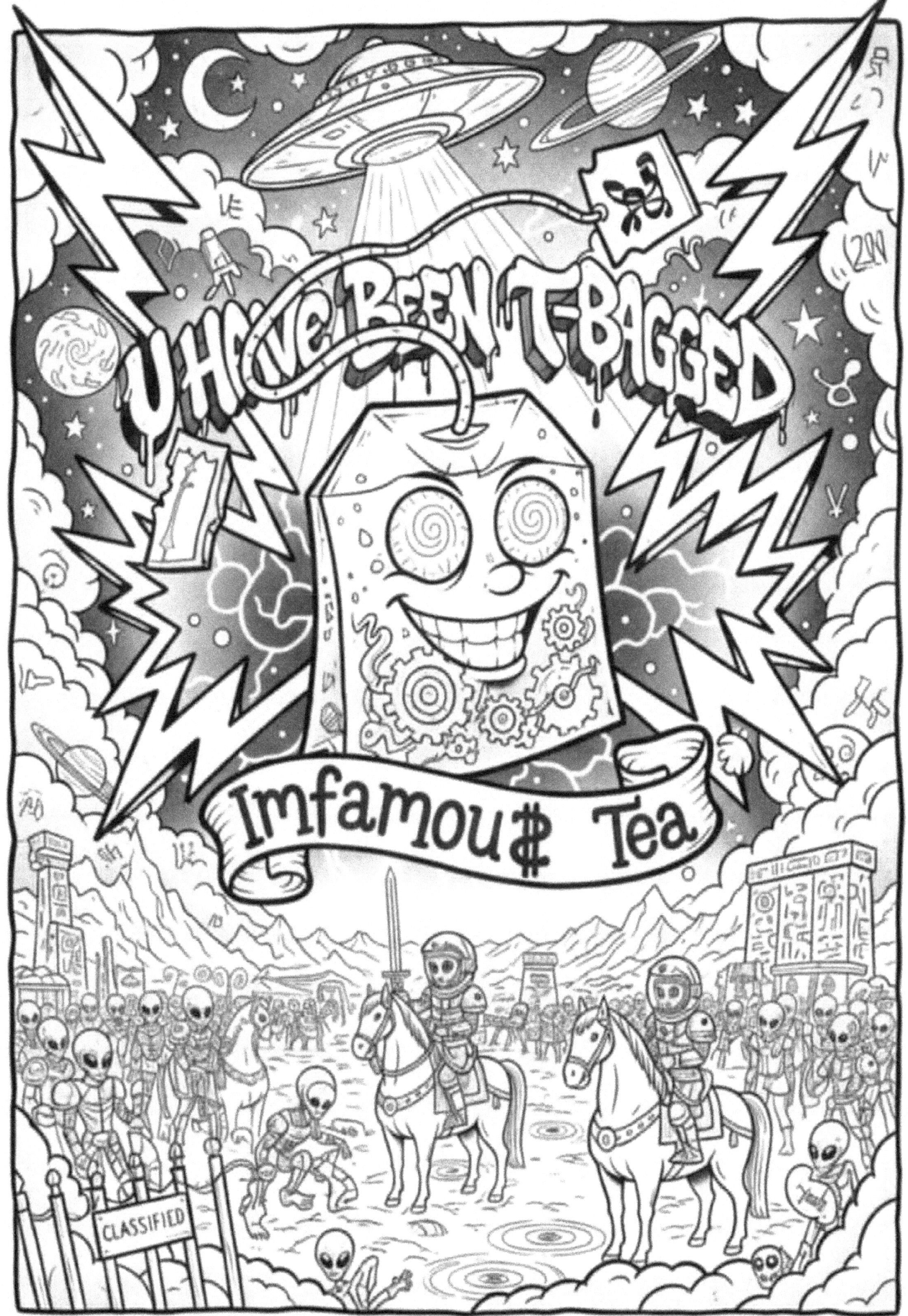
U Have Been T-Bagged
Imfamou$ Tea
CLASSIFIED

Imfamou$ Tea
HI I'M BEN
..BEN T-BAGGIE

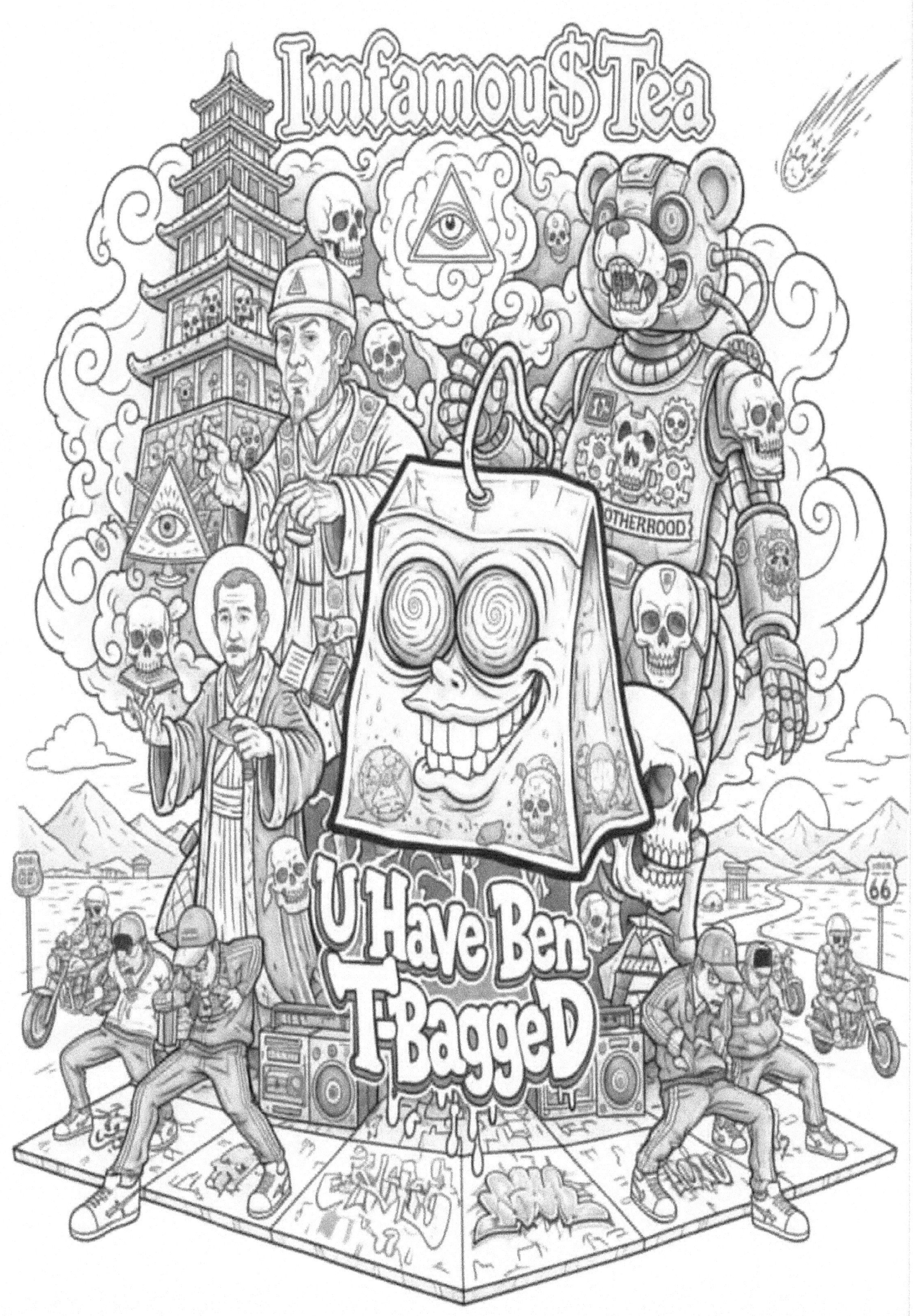
Imfamou$ Tea
OTHERROOD
U Have Ben
T-BaggeD
66

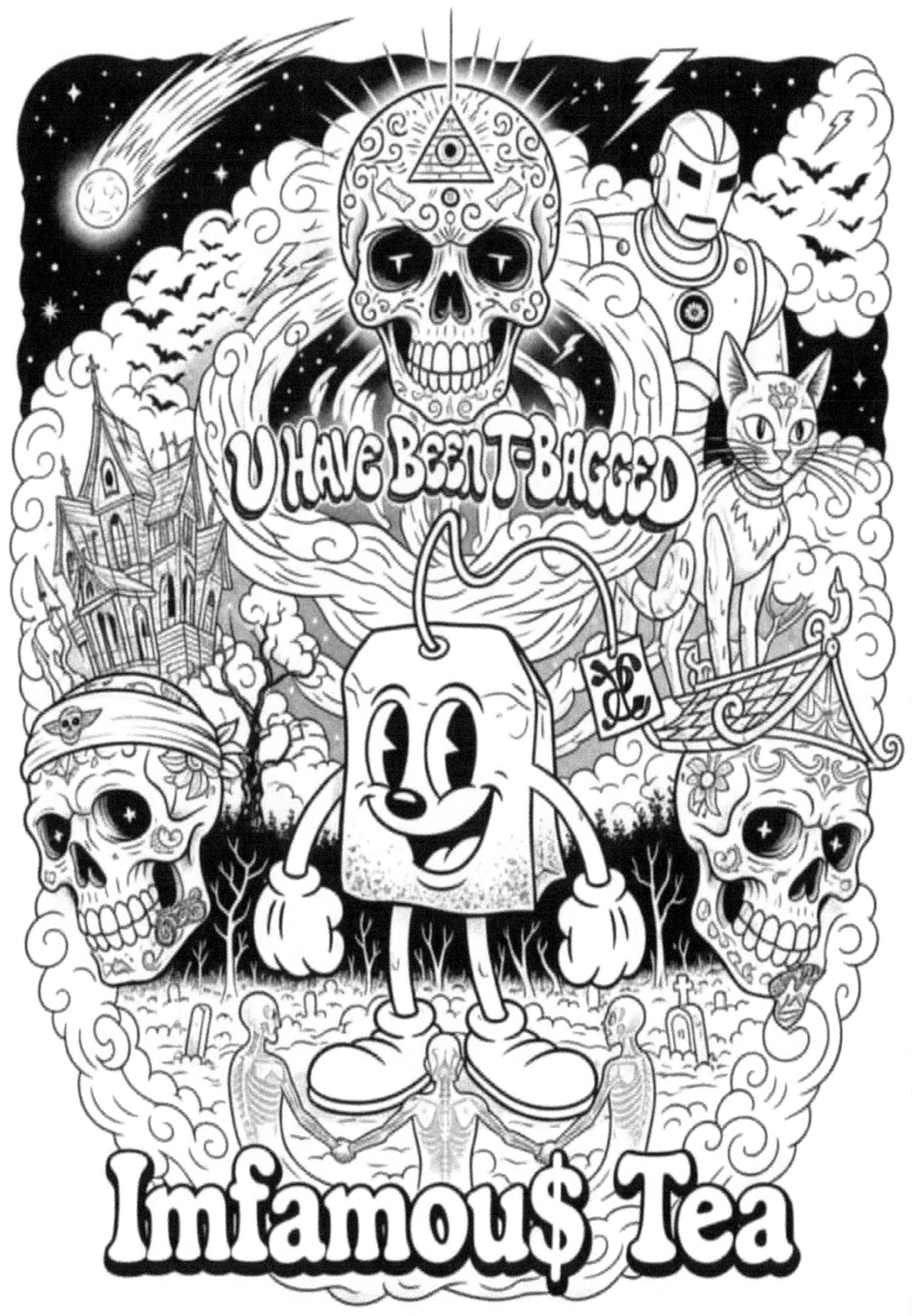
U HAVE BEEN T-BAGGED
Imfamou$ Tea

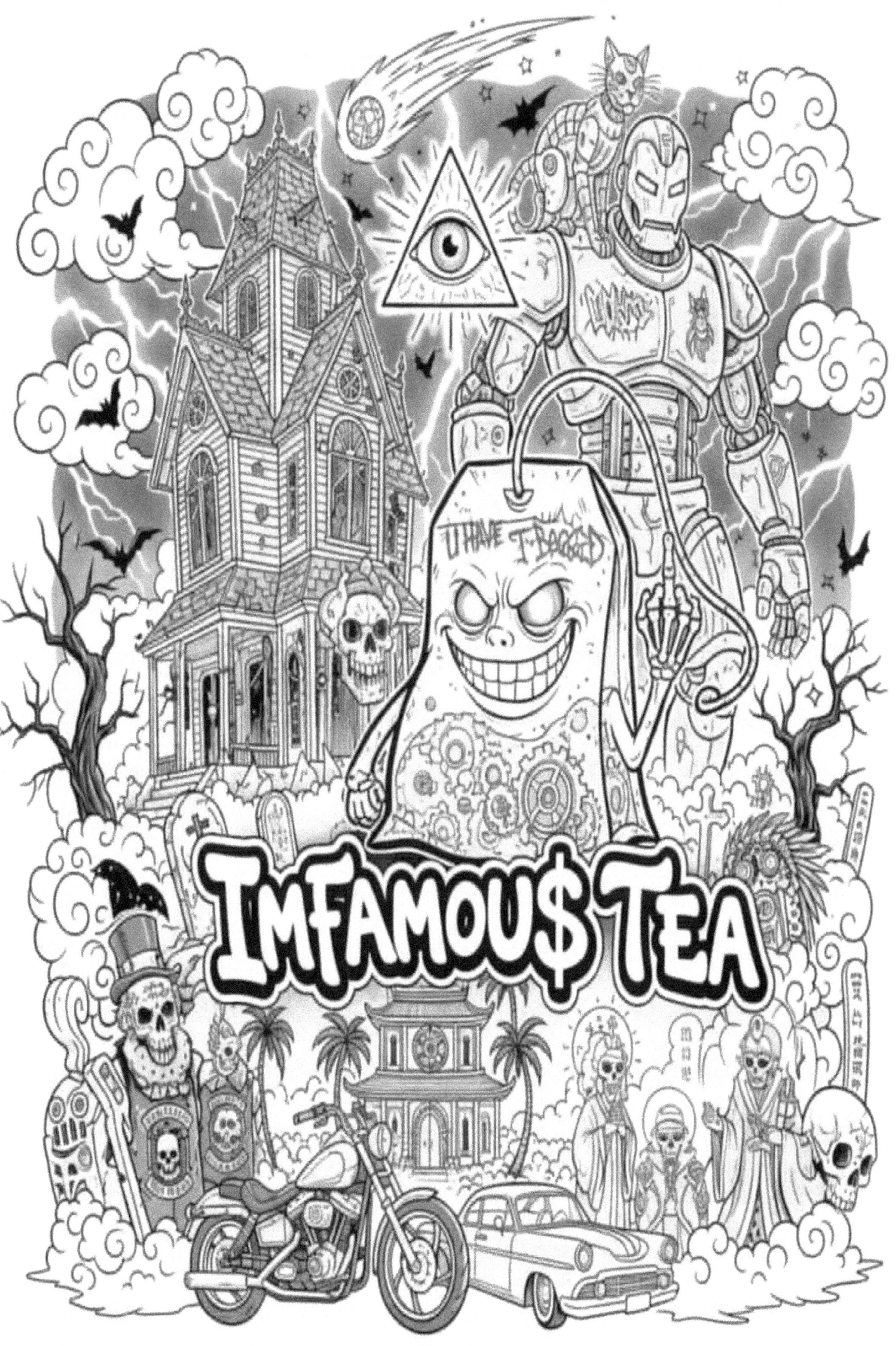
U HAVE T-BAGGED
IMFAMOU$ TEA

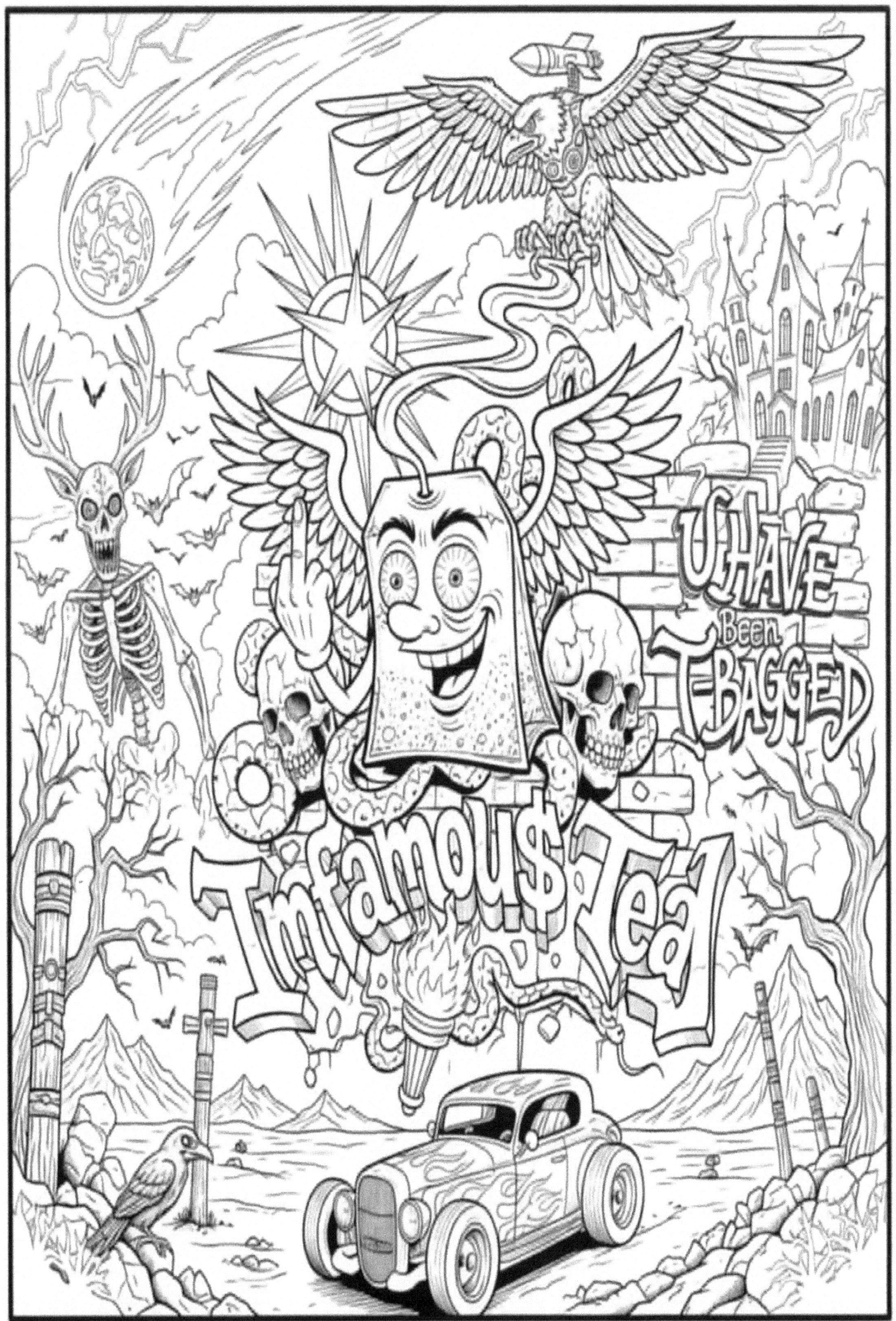
U HAVE
Been
T-BAGGED
Infamou$ Tea

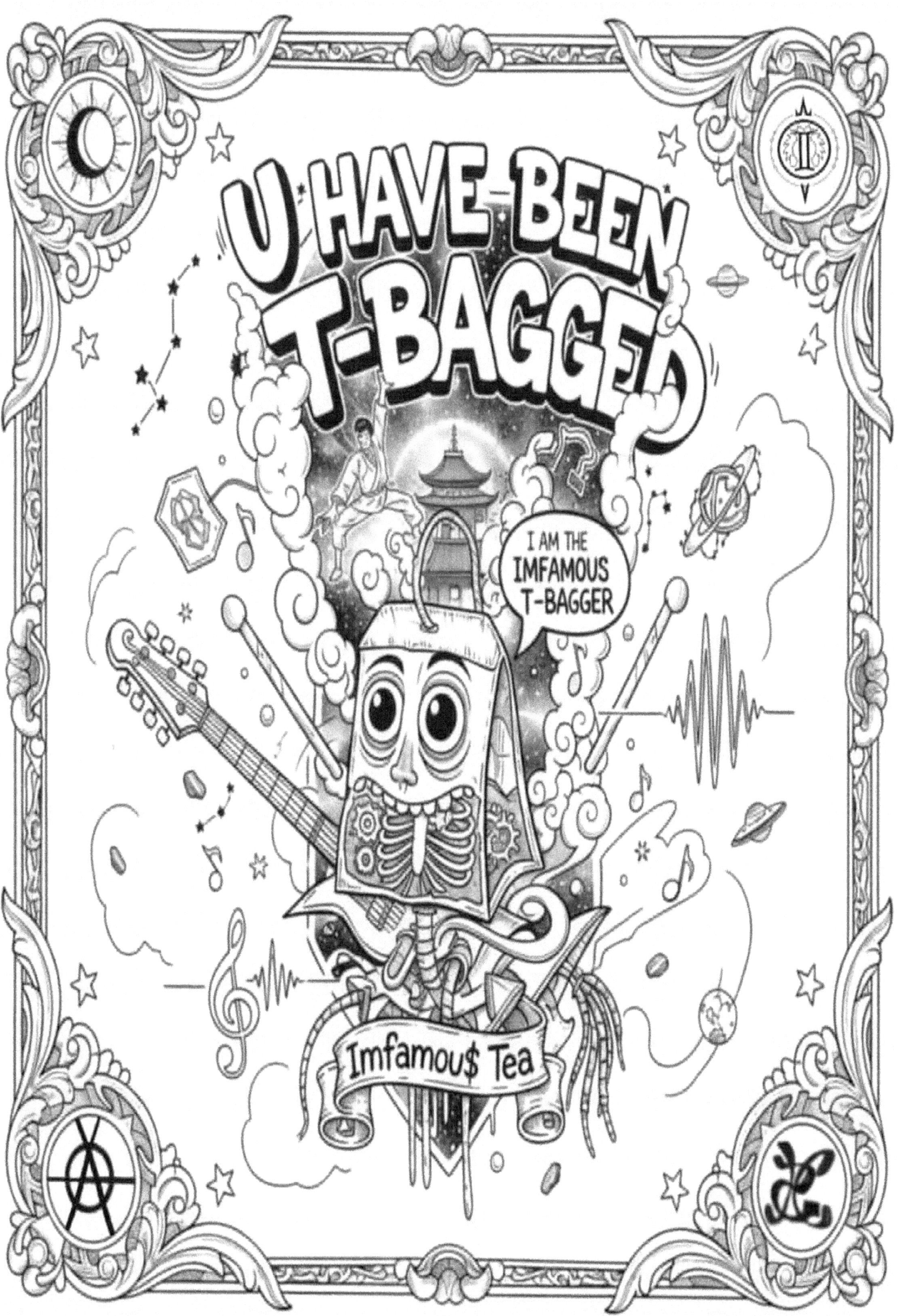
U HAVE BEEN
T-BAGGED
I AM THE
IMFAMOUS
T-BAGGER
Imfamou$ Tea

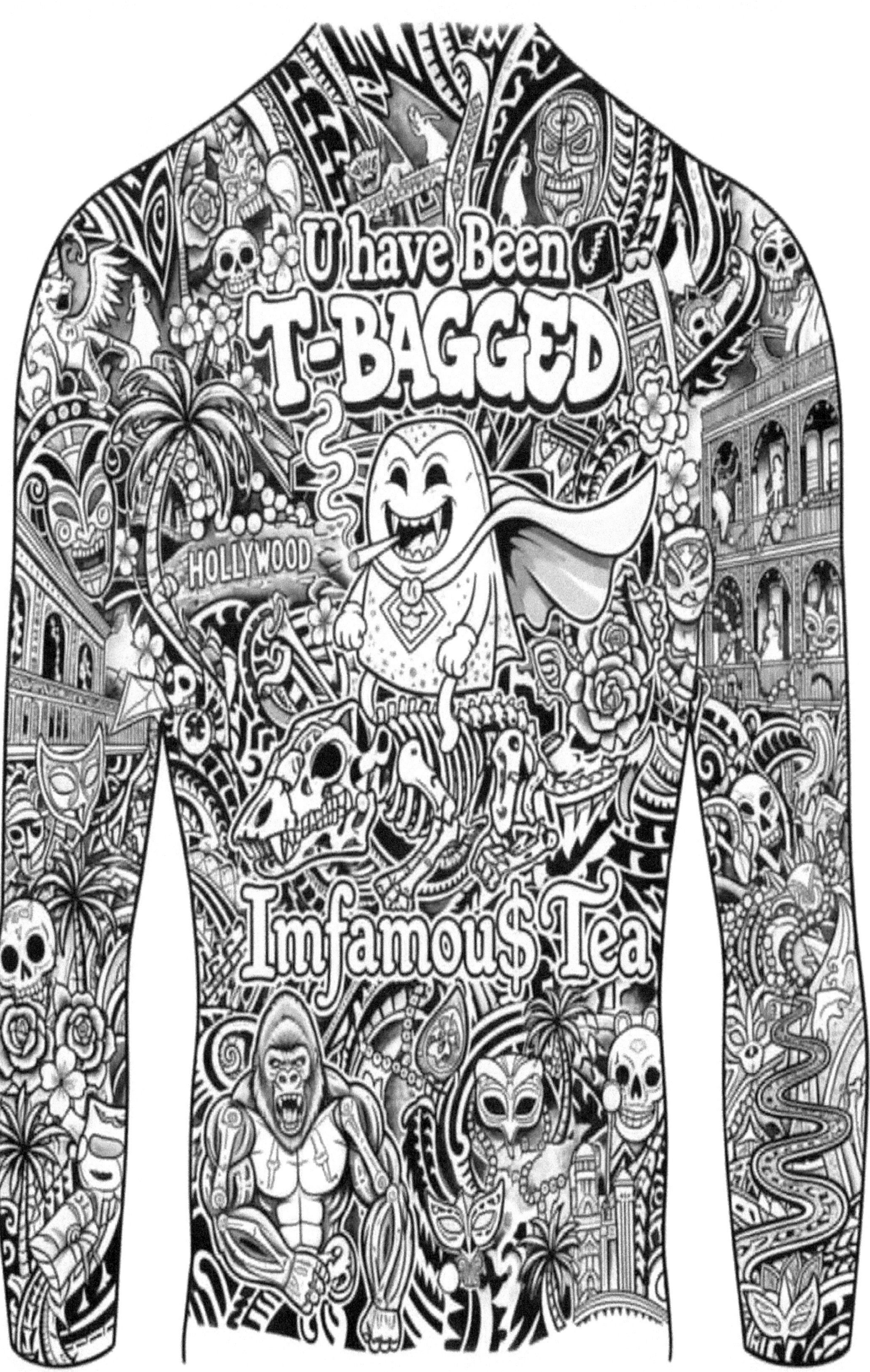
U have Been
T-BAGGED
HOLLYWOOD
Imfamou$ Tea

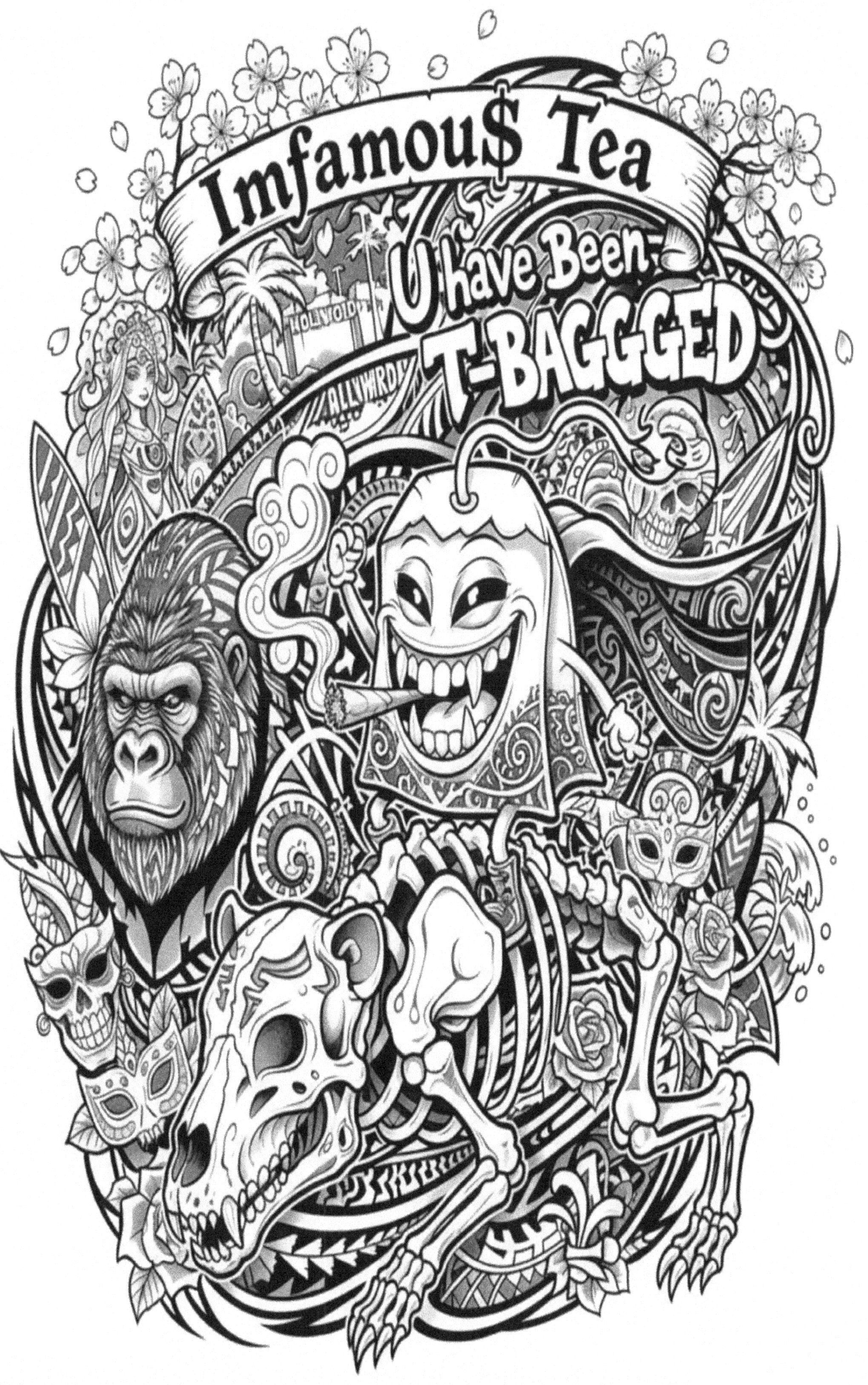
Imfamou$ Tea
U have Been
T-BAGGED

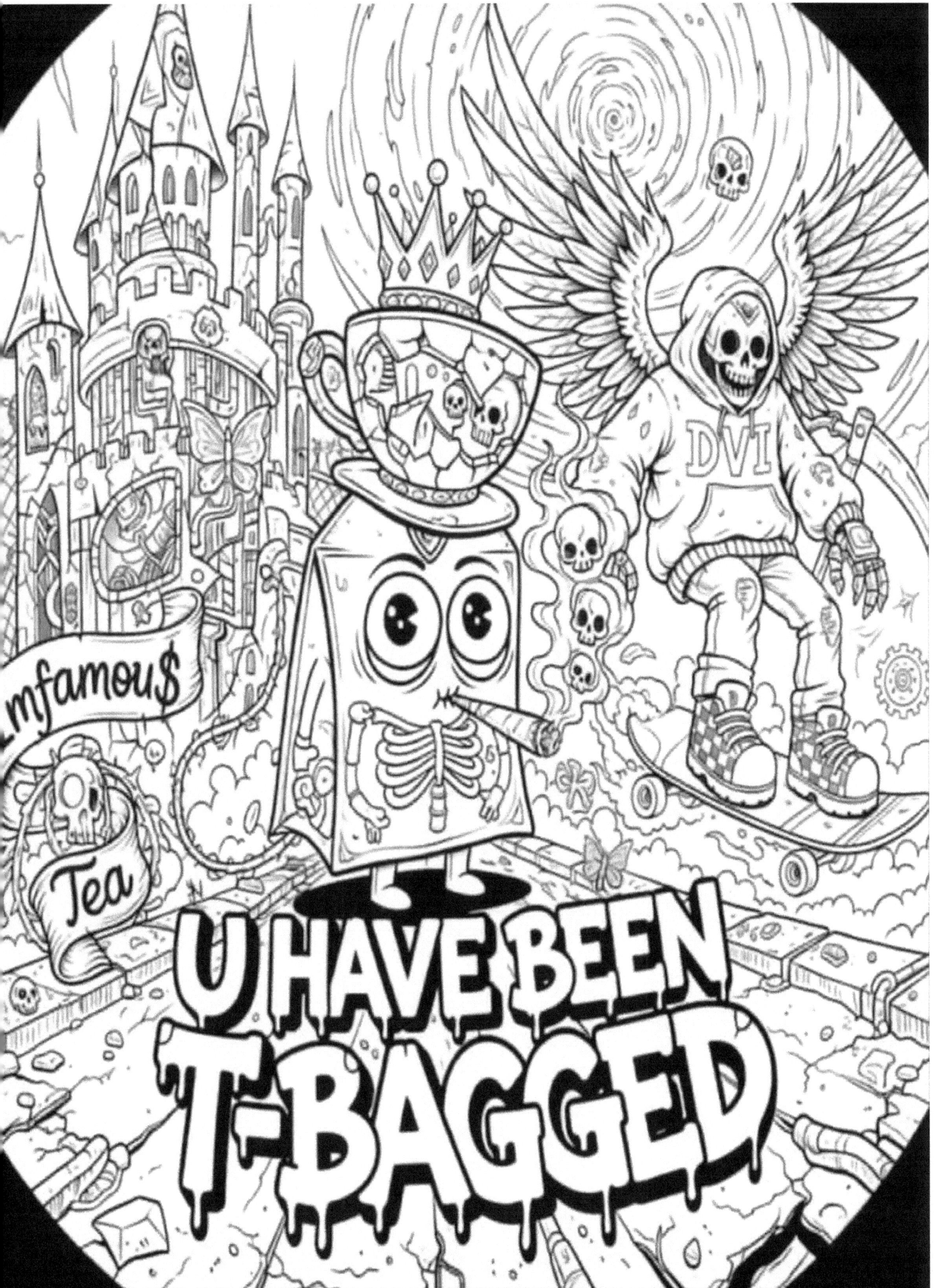
mfamou$
Tea
DVI
U HAVE BEEN
T-BAGGED

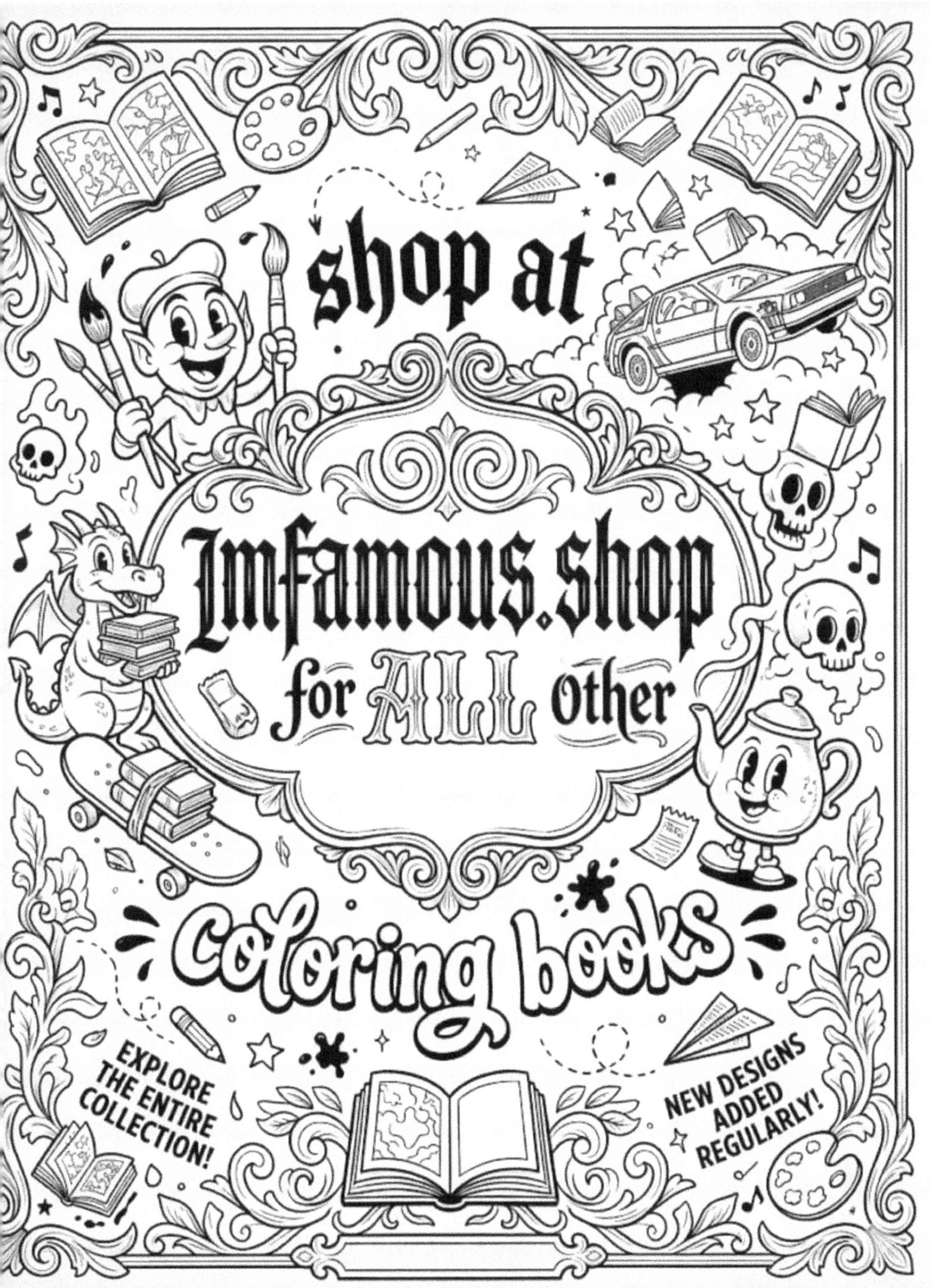
shop at
Imfamous.shop
for ALL other
coloring books
EXPLORE THE ENTIRE COLLECTION!
NEW DESIGNS ADDED REGULARLY!

# THE IMFAMOU$ MANIFESTO

THE LEGEND THE CREATOR THE NAME: RICH "IMFAMOUS" COMPTON
IN A WORLD THAT TRIES TO MAKE YOU ANONYMOUS, I CHOSE TO BE IMFAMOU$.

**RICH**: NOT JUST A NAME, BUT A BIRTHRIGHT OF ABUNDANCE--OF IDEAS, OF GRIT, AND OF TRUTH. THE NAME ITSELF MEANS KING AND LEADER.

**IMFAMOUS**: I TOOK THE "INFAMY" THE SYSTEM GAVE ME AND TURNED IT INTO AN IDEA THAT WILL ONE DAY LEAVE ITS MARK ON HISTORY AS KINGS HAVE DONE BEFORE ME.

**COMPTON**: THE SURNAME OF THE SURVIVOR. IT REPRESENTS THE "TRIPLE WRAP" AT BIRTH AND THE 33 YEARS OF STANDING SOLID WHEN OTHERS FOLDED.

**THE SIGN**: THE DOUBLE GEMINI I AM THE TWINS. ONE SIDE IS THE MASTER ARCHITECT, DRAFTING 33 PAGES OF PRECISION AND DETAIL IN THE DARK OF THE HOLE. THE OTHER SIDE IS THE SOLO KING, THE ONE WHO RUNS THE YARD, TAKES THE HIT FOR THE WEAK, AND POURS A FRESH FUCKIN CUP OF SOME GOOD OLE IMFAMOUS TEA FOR THOSE WHO CAN'T HANDLE THE HEAT. YOU DONT GET ONE WITHOUT THE OTHER SO DONT TRY AND RUN. EXCEPT WHAT IS COMING.

**THE JUNGLE**: FROM THE BAY TO THE BUSH (AT LEAST THAT'S WHAT SHE SAID HE MAY HAVE SAID THAT TOO...I BLAME THE DRUGS AND ALCOHOL AND PLEAD THE 5TH). MY JUNGLE ISNT ONE PLACE; IT'S THE PATH IVE CUT THROUGH THE WEST COAST ONE LAUGH AT A TIME. ITS THE BAY AREA HUSTLE OF FREMONT, HAYWARD, AND STOCKTON. ITS THE SANTA CRUZ MOUNTAINS OF BEN LOMOND AND FELTON. ITS THE CONCRETE CORRIDORS OF D.V.I. OLD WEST HALL, SOLANO AND HIGH DESERT STATE AND THE 23-AND-1 SILENCE OF KVSP. ITS THE "UNINCORPORATED" FREEDOM OF MODOC COUNTY AND THE HIGH DESERT OF THE OREGON BORDER. THE NIGHT SKY OF THE DARK SKY SANCTUARY AND THE LATE-NIGHT CONVERSATIONS ALONE IN THE HUMBLING PEACE AND QUIET WITH MY SPIRIT GUIDE AND SPIRITUAL TWIN METATRON.

**THE MISSION:** I PROVIDE THE UNAUTHORIZED TRUTH TO THE UNBOTHERED. WE DONT DO FLOWERS; WE DONT DO MANDALAS. WE SERVE IMFAMOUS TEA--RAW, WARPED, WITTY, A WILDLY FUNNY ART FOR THE PEOPLE WHO HAVE SEEN THE "NO OTHER CHOICE" MOMENTS AND STAYED SOLID THE ONES WHO CAN TAKE A GOOD PRANK AND LAUGH INSTEAD OF GETTING BUTT HURT OR GETTING THEIR MOIST PANTIES IN A BUNCH, OH DID I SAY MOIST, DID THAT OFFEND YOU? IF SO GO AND COLOR A T-BAG AND TAPE IT TO YOUR BESTIE'S DOOR. I SWEAR IT WILL MAKE YOU FEEL BETTER. ESPECIALLY WHEN YOU BOTH ARE LAUGHING SO HARD YOUR STOMACH HURTS OR YOU WITNESS THEM LOOSE THAT CUP OF IMFAMOUS TEA ALL DOWN THERE DUH DUN TO DUNS. THIS IS THE ART OF HUMBLING ONESELF. IN 2010, I WAS SENTENCED TO PRISON FOR A PLANT THAT IS NOW LEGAL. I DIDNT JUST SERVE THAT TIME; I USED IT TO BUILD AN EMPIRE. MY DREAM IS TO BE ONE DAY KNOWN AS THE KING OF ADULT COLORING BOOKS BECAUSE MY INK ISNT JUST PIGMENT--ITS UNIQUE ITS ORIGINAL AND ITS ONE DAY GOING TO BE PART OF HISTORY. TO THOSE WHO BELIEVE IN THE IMFAMOUS REVOLUTION, I THANK YOU! VIVA LA IMFAMOU$

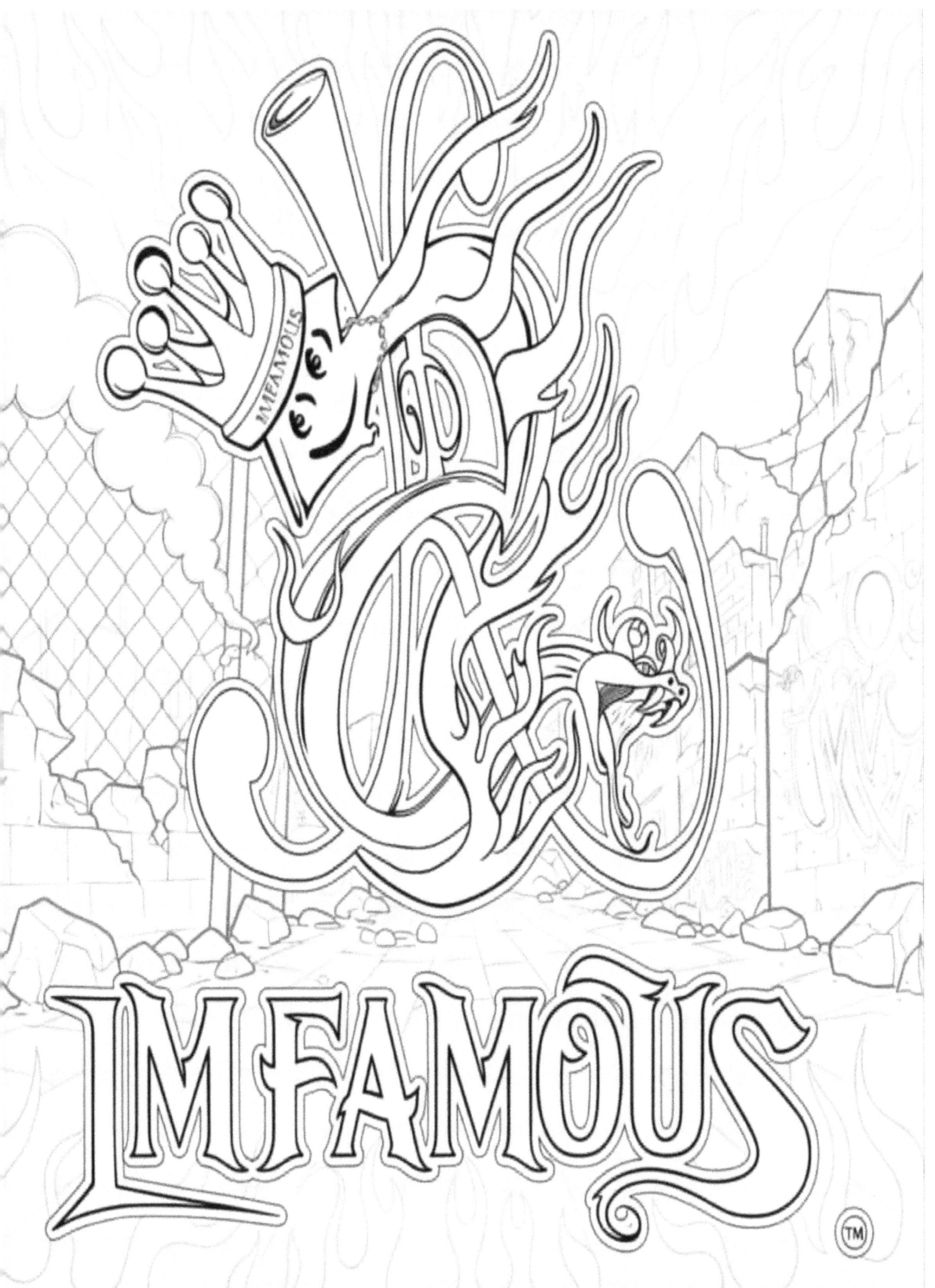
LMFAMOUS
LMFAMOUS
TM

www.ingramcontent.com/pod-product-compliance
Lightning Source LLC
Chambersburg PA
CBHW041038050726
47599CB00018B/2000

* 9 7 8 1 9 7 1 8 0 1 0 0 1 *